MW00572915

The

Four-Way
Path

life

The
Four-Way
Path

A Guide to Purushartha
and India's Spiritual Traditions
for a Life of Happiness,
Success, and Purpose

Héctor García and
Francesc Miralles

Translated by Charlotte Whittle
FOREWORD BY SHASHI THAROOR

PENGUIN LIFE

VIKING
An imprint of Penguin Random House LLC
penguinrandomhouse.com

Copyright © 2022 by Héctor García and Francesc Miralles
Translation copyright © 2024 by Charlotte Whittle
Foreword copyright © 2024 by Shashi Tharoor

Originally published in Spain as *Namasté: La vía india a la felicidad,
la realizacion y el éxito* by Ediciones Urano, Barcelona, in 2022

Illustrations copyright © 2022 by Marisa Martínez

A Penguin Life Book

LIBRARY OF CONGRESS CATALOGING-IN-PUBLICATION DATA

Names: García, Héctor, 1981– author.
Title: The four-way path : a guide to Purushartha and India's spiritual
traditions for a life of happiness, success, and purpose / Héctor
García and Francesc Miralles ; translated by Charlotte Whittle ;
foreword by Shashi Tharoor.
Other titles: Namasté. English
Description: [New York] : Penguin Life, [2024] | Originally published in
Spanish as Namasté: La vía india a la felicidad, la realizacion y el
éxito by Ediciones Urano, Barcelona, 2022. |
Includes bibliographical references.
Identifiers: LCCN 2024000417 (print) | LCCN 2024000418 (ebook) | ISBN
9780593654507 (hardcover) | ISBN 9780593654514 (ebook)
Subjects: LCSH: Purushārtha. | Spiritual life—Hinduism.
Classification: LCC BL1215.P87 G37 2024 (print) |
LCC BL1215.P87 (ebook)
LC record available at https://lccn.loc.gov/2024000417
LC ebook record available at https://lccn.loc.gov/2024000418

Printed in the United States of America
1st Printing

Designed by Cassandra Garruzzo Mueller

Contents

I.

A CULTURE OF HAPPINESS
India: The Spiritual Well of Humanity

II.

THE PHILOSOPHY OF HAPPINESS
The Indian Paths to Personal Fulfillment

III.

THE PRACTICE OF HAPPINESS
Practical Wisdom from India for Essential Well-Being

Foreword

....

This wonderful book by the authors of *Ikigai*, a world-wide bestseller about a Japanese concept that translates roughly to "the purpose of one's life," brings a similar approach to the Hindu way of life. It readably conveys some of the richness of Hindu culture and spirituality, as well as many Hindu practices like yoga, breathing, and meditation, to identify ten Indian rules for happiness that everyone can learn from and abide by.

But what does being a Hindu mean? My Hinduism is a lived faith; it is a Hinduism of experience and upbringing, a Hinduism of observation and conversation, not one anchored in deep religious study (though of course the two are not mutually exclusive). I grew up knowing few mantras, just some snatches of a couple of hymns, and practically no Sanskrit; my knowledge of Hindu sacred texts and philosophies came entirely from reading them in English translation. (When I went to a temple, I prayed in an odd combination of English, Sanskrit, and my "mother tongue," Malayalam, instinctively convinced that an omniscient God would naturally be multilingual.)

The first challenge in describing Hinduism, of course, is definitional. The name *Hindu* itself denotes something less, and more, than a set of theological beliefs. In many languages, French and Persian among them, the word for *Indian* is *Hindu*. Originally, *Hindu* simply meant the people beyond the River Sindhu, or the Indus River. But the Indus is now in Islamic Pakistan; and to make matters worse, the word *Hindu* did not exist in any Indian language until its use by foreigners gave Indians a term for self-definition. Hindus, in other words, call themselves by a label that they didn't invent in any of their own languages but adopted cheerfully when others began to refer to them by that word. (Of course, many Hindus prefer a different term altogether—*Sanatana Dharma*, or "eternal faith.")

Hinduism is thus the name that foreigners first applied to what they saw as the indigenous religion of India. It embraces an eclectic range of doctrines and practices, from pantheism to agnosticism and from faith in reincarnation to belief in the caste system. But none of these constitute an obligatory credo for a Hindu: there is none. We have no compulsory dogmas.

This is why I am more comfortable with the tenets of Hinduism than I would be with those of the other faiths of which I know. I have long thought of myself as liberal, not merely in the political sense, or even in relation to principles of economics, but also as an attitude toward life. To accept people as one finds them, to allow them to be and become what they choose, and to encourage them to do whatever they like (so long as it does not harm others) is my natural instinct. It is also what Hinduism teaches. As the great preacher Swami Vivekananda put it when he addressed the World's Parliament of Religions in Chicago in 1893, "We believe not only in universal toleration, but we accept all religions as true." He spoke for a faith that prescribes not just tolerance but also acceptance. Tolerance is essentially a patronizing virtue: the tolerant person assumes he has the truth but magnanimously is willing to allow others the right to be wrong. But the Hindu, grounded in acceptance, sees truth in all beliefs: he accepts the other's truth, demanding only that the other accept his truth. Vivekananda often quoted an ancient hymn, the "Shiva Mahimna Stotra," which declares that just as multiple rivers, originating in different places, flow down different hills and valleys, some straight, some crooked, but all end up in the same sea, so also all forms of worship reach the same divine.

Raised as I was as a Hindu, I have never found rigid and censorious beliefs appealing to my temperament. In matters of religion, too, I found my liberal instincts reinforced by the faith in which I was brought up. Hinduism is, in many ways, predicated on the idea that the eternal wisdom of the ages and of divinity cannot be confined to a single sacred book; we have many, and we can delve into each to find our own truth (or truths). As a Hindu I can claim adherence to a religion without an established church or priestly papacy, a religion whose rituals and customs I am free to reject, a religion that does not oblige me to demonstrate my faith by any visible sign, by subsuming my identity in any collective, not even by a specific day or time or frequency of worship. (There is no Hindu pope, no Hindu Vatican, no Hindu catechism, not even a Hindu Sunday.) As a Hindu I follow a faith that offers to the worshipper a veritable smorgasbord of options of divinities to adore and to pray to, of rituals to observe (or not), of customs and practices to honor (or not), of fasts to keep (or not). I subscribe to a creed that is free of the restrictive dogmas of holy writ, one that refuses to be shackled to the limitations of a single volume of holy revelation.

Hinduism professes no false certitudes. Its capacity to express wonder at creation and simultaneously skepticism about the omniscience of the Creator is unique to it. Both are captured beautifully in a verse from the thirty-five-hundred-year-old *Rig Veda*, the "Nasadiya Sukta" ("Creation Hymn"), which memorably ends:

> *Who really knows? And who can say?*
> *Whence did it all come? And how did creation happen?*
> *The gods themselves are later than creation,*
> *So who knows truly whence this great creation sprang?*
> *Who knows whence this creation had its origin?*
> *He, whether He fashioned it or whether He did not,*
> *He, who surveys it all from the highest heaven,*
> *He knows—or maybe even He does not know.*
>
> —*Rig Veda* 10.129

"Maybe even He does not know"! I love a faith that raises such a fundamental question about no less a supreme being than the Creator of the Universe himself. Maybe he does not know, indeed. Who are we mere mortals to claim a knowledge of which even he cannot be certain?

Hindu thought also makes a virtue out of the unknow-ability of God. There is a marvelous story in the Upanishads about a sage who is asked to define the nature of God; the wise man, normally loquacious, falls silent. He is pressed by his disciples for an answer, and he replies that his silence was his answer, for the Absolute is silence; the mystery of the divine reality cannot be reduced to words or speech. Neither thought nor words can suffice: "It is not understood by those who understand it," says the Kena Upanishad, "it is under-stood by those who do not understand it." The final words of the Upanishads are "neti, neti"—"not this, not this"—signifying the unspeakability of the Absolute. For many sages, their consciousness of the divine is untranslatable to others, for those who have not attained the same realization cannot grasp it through word or sign: it is "that of which nothing can be said."

In the twenty-first century, Hinduism has many of the attributes of a universal religion—a religion that is personal and individualistic, that privileges the individual and does not subordinate one to a collective; a religion that grants and respects complete freedom to the believer to find his or her own answers to the true meaning of life; a religion that offers a wide range of choice in religious practice, even in regard to the nature and form of the formless God; a religion that places great emphasis on one's mind, and values one's capacity for reflection, intellectual inquiry, and self-study; a religion that distances itself from dogma and holy writ, that is minimally prescriptive and yet offers an abundance of options, spiritual and philosophical texts, and social and cultural practices to choose from. In a world where resistance to authority is growing, Hinduism imposes no authority; in a world of networked individuals, Hinduism proposes no institutional hierarchies; in a world of open-source information sharing, Hinduism accepts all paths as equally valid; in a world of rapid transformation and accelerating change, Hinduism is adaptable and flexible, which is why it has survived for millennia.

Above all, as a Hindu I belong to the only major religion in the world that does not claim to be the only true religion. I find it immensely congenial to be able to face my fellow human beings of other faiths without being burdened by the conviction that I am embarked upon a "true path" that they have missed. Hinduism asserts that all ways of belief are equally valid, and Hindus readily venerate the saints and the sacred objects of other faiths. I am proud that I can honor the sanctity of other faiths without feeling I am betraying my own.

It is very much in the same spirit that Héctor García and

Francesc Miralles have approached this book. They have done a marvelous job of identifying principles, practices, and prescriptions for living from this extraordinary faith, its spiritual and doctrinal offshoots, and the culture it has sustained for five thousand years. I commend their book for delving so accessibly into the complex cultural and spiritual traditions of India, and distilling from them guides for living that should be valuable to everyone with an open mind and a willingness to learn from the wisdom of the ancients.

SHASHI THAROOR

The Geography of Happiness

This book drinks from a well of wisdom as ancient as human culture and contains the keys for giving shape as much to the present as to the future we all dream of.

When we decided to write it, our books had already been translated into more than sixty languages and had been number-one bestsellers all over the world. The most recent phase of the *Ikigai* phenomenon is in India, where our book has been the bestselling title two years in a row. This led us to travel to the Indian subcontinent, the cradle of spirituality, to speak, attend festivals, and give interviews.

In addition to telling us what our work had meant to them, kind readers we met on our travels often asked us why we didn't write a book inspired by Indian wisdom.

Each time we spoke of the possibility, it seemed to us like an enormous, ambitious, and thrilling challenge. India is not just a country with a young, proactive, and forward-looking population, as well as the largest democracy on the planet. It is also the home of some of the oldest and greatest spiritual traditions that have shaped humanity. Better still, it has the potential to bring happiness to the whole world, if we return to these origins.

Visitors to India are surprised to encounter such cultural diversity in a single place: colorful Hindu temples, churches in Goa and Kerala, sublime mosques like the one in New Delhi and the Islamic mausoleum of the Taj Mahal. In its streets pulsing with life, they will find Jain mystics, Christian monks, elegant Sikhs wearing turbans, and the sadhus who roam the country making pilgrimages in preparation for death.

One gets the impression that the entire world, at least as far as spirituality goes, is here.

If we look back, we'll see that Siddhartha Gautama, who would later become the Buddha, began his discoveries to the north of India. A millennium earlier, we find the Vedas, the four most ancient texts in Indian literature, which gave shape to Hinduism.

Many mindfulness practices popular in the West, like yoga and meditation, originate in India, in addition to concepts such as karma and ancestral healing practices such as Ayurveda.

India is the future of the world. The current CEOs of Microsoft and Google, among other multinationals, come from this culture full of brilliant mathematicians, programmers, and engineers. What is the secret to their success?

In these pages, we will find out.

It is hard not to be impressed by the fount of endless riches that is India. Our mission was to write a short, fresh, illuminating book that provides answers to today's challenges in the wake of the pandemic's ravages.

The questions that we ask ourselves today are ones that Indian mystics have been asking themselves for the past five thousand years:

- How can we leave suffering behind and start to lead a fulfilling existence?
- What ways do we have of awakening all the dormant creative energy inside us?
- Can we make the law of karma work in our favor in our daily lives?
- What are the best techniques for freeing ourselves from stress, anxiety, and fear?

- How can we care for body, mind, and spirit and be full of energy until the end of our lives?

To answer these questions and many others in a useful and practical way, we have turned to humanity's best teachers in the art of happiness and personal fulfillment.

From thousand-year-old wise men to modern figures like Ramana Maharshi and Jiddu Krishnamurti, India offers a wealth of inspiration to help us break through when we are stuck, develop all our capacities, and become fully realized.

In the following pages, you will embark on a journey to discover the Indian way to happiness. Its infinite paths can change more than just our lives. They can also change the future.

As we will see throughout this book, tomorrow is a product of the rituals, attitudes, and actions we practice today.

Our purpose is to build the best possible future, starting now. For you and for the world you are creating.

HÉCTOR GARCÍA AND FRANCESC MIRALLES

I

A CULTURE
OF HAPPINESS

....

India: The Spiritual
Well of Humanity

Purushartha

....

Why do you think the Japanese concept of *ikigai—* your reason for being—is so popular in India?" is one of the questions we get asked the most from all over the world. Our intuition told us that there must be something in common between the Japanese way of life and the Indian way of life, so we've responded to the question by saying: "Indian culture is the wellspring from which many Japanese traditions emerged a long time ago. It seems that people in both Japan and India consider the purpose of our lives to be of utter importance."

But in our quest to understand how to have a good life, and the role of one's purpose in it, we pursued a more concrete answer.

After reading dozens of books on Indian culture and traveling around India talking with thousands of readers of our previous books, we encountered a key concept from Hinduism: *purushartha*.

It can be translated as "the objective of human beings" or as "the purpose or goal of a human being."

Purushartha (पुरुषार्थ) is a Sanskrit word made up of two parts:

PURUSHA (पुरुष): "spirit" or "immaterial essence of a human"

ARTHA (अर्थ): "meaning," "purpose," "objective," or "goal"

In order to live in accordance with purushartha and to have a fulfilling life, there are four areas—known as the four purusharthas—that we need to cultivate:

- *Kama* refers to the pleasures of the senses and the enjoyment of what is beautiful in life. It is also about desires, emotions, and love.
  - You can ask yourself: What do I love doing? What do I want?
- *Dharma* is a word that has many meanings. At a very general level it means "what makes the Universe exist," "the right way of living," or "the eternal nature of

reality." It includes the moral values, duties, rights, and virtues that each individual pursues in order for harmony to prevail in the world and in order to realize one's true nature.

- You can ask yourself: What does the world need from me? Why do I exist?

- *Artha* is what you need to do in order to sustain your life. It is about bringing prosperity to yourself, your family, and your community. In a modern sense it is about your job, your career, your financial security, and wealth in general.

  - You can ask yourself: What do I need to sustain my life? What can bring wealth to me and my loved ones?

- *Moksha* means self-realization, liberation, and freedom. In some schools of thought we reach a state of moksha when we are free from death and rebirth. In others it means simply being in a state in which you have the freedom to work on your self-realization. In modern terms it could be associated with the top of Abraham Maslow's hierarchy of needs. Who are you in your most essential sense? Try to think how you would define yourself without mentioning your name, your job, things you identify with, your country . . .

• You can ask yourself: Who am I? Who am I
  in the truest sense?

We arranged these four purusharthas in a Venn diagram,
just like we did for ikigai, and noticed that purushartha
and ikigai are very similar. What a pleasant surprise! The
wisdom and tools to achieve a life of meaning and purpose
have been available to the people of the Indian subcontinent for a very long time.

DHARMA
What does the world
need from me?

MOKSHA
Who am I?

PURUSHARTHA
What is my purpose?

ARTHA
What do I need
to sustain my life?

KAMA
What do
I love doing?

Why am I alive? What should I do with my life? What is
my purpose? The answers to these questions can be found
in the timeless wisdom of the ancient texts, philosophers,
and traditions of India.

We wanted to learn more from India and share what we learned with our readers. The lessons apply to all of us, whether you believe in the afterlife, in no god or one god or multiple gods, or in any particular religion.

There is one thing all of us, as humans, can agree on:

At this moment, while you are reading these words, you are a human being who is alive. And while alive, you should aim to have a purposeful life and bring purpose to your people, your family, your friends, your community, your country or region, and all the world.

You might already know what your purpose in life is, or you might not yet know. If you already know, this book provides a blueprint for living in accordance with your purushartha. If you don't yet know, it will give you the tools to start the adventure of knowing yourself better and discovering your purpose.

The Doors to Wisdom

....

I t is estimated that as of the year 2024, India will be the country with the highest number of inhabitants in the world, with around 17 percent of the total population of the planet. And according to various studies, this will remain the case for the rest of the twenty-first century.

For many centuries, the Indian subcontinent was known as Hindustan—named after the Indus River—until it became a British colony and the period of the Raj began. Today, the name Hindustan has fallen into relative disuse.

Since the partition of India in 1947, this vast region has been divided over time into different countries: Bhutan, Bangladesh, India, Nepal, Pakistan, and Sri Lanka. In this book we will sometimes use *Indian civilization*, *Hindustan*, and the *Indian subcontinent* as synonyms to refer to different aspects of the shared past of those territories' inhabitants, who have influenced with their culture and ideas not just a large part of Asia but also the whole world.

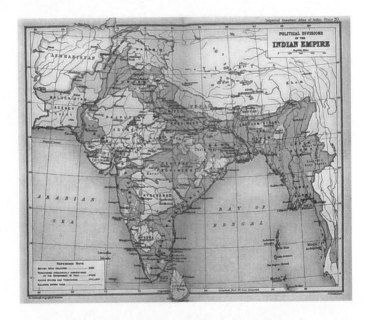

Map of the British Indian Empire published in the 1909 edition of *The Imperial Gazetteer of India*, where the regions together are approximately equivalent to what today is considered the Indian subcontinent, historically known as Hindustan

In terms of economic power, it is also crucial to understand that the peoples of India were world leaders from the first to the seventeenth centuries. During these seventeen centuries, the territory was the greatest economic power on the planet in terms of gross domestic product. In some periods, more than 25 percent of the global economy was concentrated in this region.

While other places slept through the medieval era, India prospered.

From the seventeenth century until a large part of the twentieth century, India went into economic decline. Yet fortunately, it has seen progress as much in its gross domestic product as in the living standards of its inhabitants, especially in the most recent decades. It is currently the fifth largest economy in the world, and if it continues to develop at the present rate, there is no doubt that it will become one of the three largest economies on the planet in the next few decades.

Why have the prosperity, cultural riches, and history of Hindustan often been forgotten?

We are convinced that India will return to its position of global leadership, and this book is our small contribution to making the secrets of its culture known.

In the nineteenth century, the French writer Victor Hugo wrote, "An invasion of armies can be resisted, but not an idea whose time has come." In 1991, the Indian minister of finance Manmohan Singh, who would go on to become the prime minister, quoted Hugo and then said: "Let the whole world hear it loud and clear. India is now wide awake."

Though India is destined to be the business and technological power of the future, as we will see in the chapter dedicated to new leaders, it has always been the center of the spiritual world.

For millennia, its mystics and scholars have been pioneers in matters that have come to be studied in the modern field of psychology. In times when life meant little more than survival in most of the world, consciousness had already awakened in the Indian subcontinent.

In the year 327 BC, Alexander the Great arrived in India, entering through modern-day Punjab, but the relationship between India and the West goes back much further than most people realize. India has been radiating its light to the rest of the planet for millennia.

DID JESUS DIE IN KASHMIR?

Among the most intriguing conspiracy theories about the East-West spiritual connection is the legend, recounted, for example, by Andreas Faber Kaiser in his book *Jesus Died in Kashmir: Jesus, Moses and the Ten Lost Tribes of Israel*, that Jesus of Nazareth did not die on the cross. Instead, after his wounds were healed, he was freed and set out on a pilgrimage to the East, following the trail of the lost tribes of Israel, which led him to live in India until he was advanced in age.

In Srinagar, the summer capital of Jammu and Kashmir, one can visit the tomb of a pilgrim buried around the year 100 who, according to accounts from the period, not only wore a white tunic but also had wounds on his hands and feet and arrived in the company of a woman named Marjan, who may have been Mary Magdalene.

Five Teachers and Five Ideas for the World Today

Before going into concrete aspects of Indian spirituality to guide us in the art of happiness, in this chapter we will take a brief tour of a few teachers and ideas still relevant today.

1. **Parshva: "Every living thing has a soul."** In the eighth century BC, this prophet, little known in the West, was a preacher of Jainism—the oldest Indian religion after the Vedic texts—which today boasts six million followers. A son of kings, like the Buddha, he maintained that there is no holiness other than life itself, which permeates everything.

Many Jains therefore sweep the floor and wear masks, to avoid stepping on or swallowing insects. The very concept of *ahimsa*, the nonviolence that Gandhi practiced in his campaign to liberate India, is based on this religion.

2. **Buddha: "Pain is inevitable, but suffering is optional."** This may be the most well-known insight of Siddhartha Gautama, the prince who set out to find a solution to human suffering in the sixth and fifth centuries BC. Things that happen to us, like pleasure and pain, are one thing; our interpretation of them, or reaction to reality, is another. Therein lies the key to human freedom.

3. **Mahavira: "If you know the way, you know the destination since the destination is not at the end; in every moment and every step there is the destination, it is in the awareness of now."** This insight, from the fifth century BC's spiritual heir to Parshva, sounds very current. Mahavira was a wanderer born in a palace, like his teacher, and his words could have been taken from Eckhart Tolle's *The Power of Now*, except that they were uttered two and a half millennia earlier. Mahavira emphasized that the spiritual path is

not mapped but invisible, and that therefore no one can travel it on your behalf.

4. **Patanjali: "When you are inspired by some great purpose, some extraordinary project, all your thoughts break their bonds: Your mind transcends limitations, your consciousness expands in every direction, and you find yourself in a new, great, and wonderful world. Dormant forces, faculties, and talents become alive, and you discover yourself to be a greater person by far than you ever dreamed yourself to be."** We have jumped to the second or third century, when it's believed the author of the *Yoga Sutras*—a Sanskrit text that forms the philosophical basis of yoga— lived. From his luminous past he speaks of essential human purpose and goals (purushartha) and even precisely describes the theory of flow, popularized by Mihaly Csikszentmihalyi.

5. **Ramakrishna: "The fabled musk deer searches the world over for the source of the scent that comes from itself."** We will end with an icon much closer to us in time. Born in 1836 and dead fifty years later, Sri Ramakrishna was perhaps the pioneer of the modern teachers. Thanks to an article in

a newspaper, he became a celebrity all over Calcutta, where he met the young poet Rabindranath Tagore. He maintained that all beliefs and religions lead to God if you are willing to realize the final truth.

Each of these teachers represents a door into the future, since they anticipated questions of consciousness that today are the foundation of personal development.

The Blind Men and the Elephant

This is one of the oldest philosophical parables in Indian culture. A multitude of versions have been written, some of the most famous being those of Ramakrishna and of the poet John Godfrey Saxe. This is our version.

An elephant arrived in a small village, and four blind men gathered to examine it. The first man touched its trunk and exclaimed in fright, "It's a giant snake!" But this did not discourage the others, who were bold enough to touch other parts of it. "This isn't an animal—it's clearly a tree trunk," said the second man, touching one of the elephant's legs. The third blind man stroked one of the ears and said, "You are mistaken—this is a fan." Finally, the fourth observed the polished texture of one of the tusks and announced, "What I am touching is hard and smooth like a spear."

To resolve the disagreement, a villager who could see explained: "You are all somewhat right, but you have described only parts of the truth without understanding the essence of what they are when they are together. The elephant is not a snake, nor a tree, nor a fan, nor a spear. It is an animal with a trunk, tusks, and enormous ears and feet. We are all blind in one way or another. We should let this be a life lesson: if we want to know the truth, we must converse with an open mind rather than simply asserting our own opinions."

In this traditional story, none of the blind men have seen the elephant, yet they still dare to express their views and are convinced that their perspective is the correct one. The message is that no matter how convinced we are of something, others who believe the opposite will also be convinced that they are right. The truth belongs to no one.

Science, Truth, and Life

In the scientific world, analogies resembling this parable are used to investigate supposed truths seen by the naked eye and the methods of experts in a single field.

For example, Werner Heisenberg, the 1932 Nobel Prize laureate in physics and considered one of the pioneers of quantum mechanics, warned, "The measuring device has been constructed by the observer, and we have to remember that what we observe is not nature in itself but nature exposed to our method of questioning."

Usually when a scientific field comes up against obstacles, different groups of scientists maintain different hypotheses, but no one manages to demonstrate which is correct. Those who are able to make great contributions and become part of the history of science integrate various hypotheses into a single theory, thus eliminating the contradictions among them.

Beyond science, the parable of the elephant can be applied to our lives through the following three routes.

THE PATH TO TRUTH

- To approach truth, we cannot trust one single opinion— not even our own. We must open ourselves up to a wider range of possibilities and combine apparently contradictory perspectives.
- If we keep our minds open to the opinions of others, taking advantage of their knowledge, we will be able to broaden our own version of truth.

COMMUNICATION AND COLLABORATION

- We must not assume that other people are wrong. It is better to assume that, from their point of view, we are the ones who are wrong.
- As Don Miguel Ruiz, the author of *The Four Agreements*, would say, do not assume that others have bad intentions.

- Dialogue with others will give us a more complete, more global outlook.

The Parts and the Whole

- Knowing something does not mean that we understand it completely. We are often exposed only to parts of the truth, just like the blind men in the fable.
- The more parts of and perspectives on a problem we know, the closer we will be to solving it.

We will end with a famous quote that reinforces the fable: "The whole is greater than the sum of its parts."

Torii and Torana

Closed minds tend to focus only on the differences between one culture and another, and are likely to use hackneyed phrases like "There's nowhere else like X." But it has always seemed more interesting to us to observe what unites us. In the end, we are all human beings sharing space on this enormous rock revolving around a star.

One of the best ways to open our mind and not limit

ourselves to seeing only one part of the elephant is to travel. In fact, the origin of the book you are reading, just like our previous books, lies in our travels through Asia.

Travel helps cultivate humility. It allows you to realize that perhaps the customs and traditions of the place where you live are neither the best ones nor the only ones.

For example, one of the symbols of Japan are the torii gates. These slender constructions mark the entrance to sacred ground. The world's oldest torii that historians have verified was built in 992 BC at a shrine in Osaka.

After eighteen years living in Japan, Héctor believed that torii were a unique feature of Japanese culture. But when we traveled to India at the end of 2019, we discovered that there had already been similar gates called *torana* in Indian lands long before the first Japanese torii.

In addition to both words beginning with *tor-*, the torii at the entrance to Japanese shrines and the torana found in India have a shared simplicity of structure. They are usually made up of two posts driven into the ground and one or several transversal beams uniting the posts in the form of an arch.

Torii (鳥居) in Japanese means "place where birds perch." In Shintoism, birds are believed to be messengers from the gods.

Torana (तोरण) in Sanskrit means "arch."

Torii

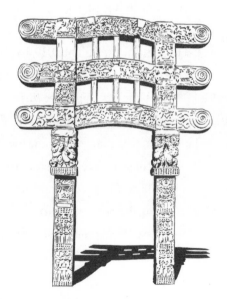

Torana

The purpose of both the torii and the torana is to mark the entrance to a sacred space. Both structures indicate the importance of the transition from the worldly to the sacred and vice versa.

Might the Japanese torii have been inspired by the Indian torana? Historians still debate this, but all signs point to a clear influence.

This is one of many observations that show us that Indian culture is far more influential than we had imagined.

The Alchemy of Travel

Travel helps us broaden our perspective, making us realize, among other things, that what we believe to be "ours" really is not. Nearly everything is a product of the evolution and mixing of the cultures and peoples of the whole world.

The fish that has never leapt above the surface of the lake does not really know where it is. It is difficult to understand our own culture if we are always immersed in it.

The purpose of travel is not simply to arrive at your destination and take photos. A real trip is a transformative experience. After this kind of trip, we return home as different people. We have installed new software in our minds that will help us empathize more with others and live our lives with a more global and humane perspective.

This is also the purpose of spirituality: to widen the bandwidth of our minds.

At the end of the day, life is a journey. There is no point in having a fixed destination in mind; it is much better to want to discover who we are along the way.

RULES FOR THE SPIRITUAL TRAVELER

1. Avoid traveling just to put a flag on the map and say, "I was here."
2. Leave your prejudices and preconceived ideas at home. Do not judge but learn along the way.
3. Do not be guided by the "must-sees" in every place. Allow your feet to take you places that don't appear on the map.
4. Look, listen, smell, taste, touch . . . feel!
5. Mix with the locals to experience life like those who live there.
6. Getting lost can be a path to the greatest discoveries.
7. The soul of a place is in its people, not its monuments.
8. Travel with words: get hold of books about places

you'd like to see. The pleasure of travel begins in the preparations.

9. Always take a notebook and something to write with. Your next adventure might inspire you to write a book.

10. Learn some of the language. Even if it's only a dozen words, it is a sign of respect toward the locals and will help you connect with them.

The following quote is sometimes attributed to the prophet Mohammed: "Do not tell me what you have studied, tell me how much you have traveled." As far as the art of travel is concerned, India is undoubtedly the best university.

Countless Western intellectuals have flocked to this part of the world in search of guidance and change. Martin Luther King himself said, "To other countries I may go as a tourist, but to India I come as a pilgrim."

Let's continue our pilgrimage!

The Way of the Sadhu

....

If we are to speak of travelers and pilgrims, it is impossible not to spend a chapter walking alongside the sadhus, the holiest people on earth according to Hinduism. Their way of life, based on renunciation as a path to spiritual clarity, is a choice as extraordinary as it is surprising to the Western eye.

The goal of sadhus is clear: to focus their efforts on the fourth purushartha (moksha) in order to achieve enlightenment by cleansing their karma to escape the wheel of *samsara*, or the cycle of successive reincarnations.

To attain wisdom—*sadhu* literally means "a good, virtuous, honest, chaste man"—they will have to free themselves completely from temptation and worldly desires, requiring that they leave behind all possessions and emotional bonds.

This kind of existence can seem limited, but it's one of supreme inner riches—sadhus' lifelong pilgrimage affords them profound self-knowledge. In the words of the religious teacher Swami Vivekananda, "He who has no faith in himself can never have faith in God."

The Four Phases of Life

In both India and Nepal, we can recognize sadhus stationed near a temple or sitting beneath a tree or in a cave, dressed in white or saffron. Some are almost or completely naked, accompanied only by a bowl for drinking water or collecting alms and a small bundle that might include sacred texts and certain items that distinguish them as members of a specific sect of sadhus. It is customary to see them with their faces painted or covered in ash and their hair matted into *jatas* (dreadlocks), and with bushy white beards.

The sadhus might be mistaken for vagrants, but in India they are venerated and respected for their prayers and blessings, and because special powers are attributed to them, from the feared evil eye to levitation.

They live on donated food and money, and may also offer spiritual consolation and guidance as fruits of their meditation, palm reading and fortune telling, amulets, potions, herbal medicines, and songs.

Most sadhus move among the seven sacred places (the Sapta Puri; the most famous is the city of Varanasi, or Benares) in an ongoing pilgrimage, so as not to lose momentum. Others are more sedentary and live with their religious orders in monasteries (*mathas*).

Many of these eternal pilgrims were previously men of significant means. How did they decide to live a life of asceticism as sadhus?

It is estimated that between four and five million Indians embark on a path to divinity. Some 10 percent of them are holy women known as *sadhvis* or *aryikas*. They might be devoted to Shiva and be known as Shaivites or Saivas, who wear a U and a dot painted in the center of their foreheads; or they might worship Vishnu and be known as Vaishnavites or Vaishnavas, who wear three vertical stripes in the same place on their faces. The female deity Shakti can also be an object of veneration for the sadhus.

But it is Shiva, who dwells in Mount Kailash in Tibet, who is most venerated by sadhus and sadhvis.

To reach the wisdom that flows from the gods, the Hindu tradition explains that life has four phases:

1. *Brahmacharya*, or preparation and study in childhood and adolescence

2. *Grihastha*, or starting and supporting a family in adulthood
3. *Vanaprastha*, or pilgrimage, once family obligations have been fulfilled
4. *Sannyasa*, or the search for true meaning, which involves cutting ties with worldly, material things to rise toward the spiritual plane

Sadhvis can move toward the fourth phase when they are widowed. Widows used to be invisible and disdained in Indian society. Today they can embark on a path of holy renunciation, or *sadhana*. And while sadhus used to be limited to members of the Brahman caste, now they come from every social background and level of education. All of them commit to the total abandonment of any kind of attachment and, in accordance with the teachings of Swami Sivananda, of a life without any desire to be happy.

TOUCHING THE SKY

One of the most famous sadhus of modern times is Amar Bharati, who in the early 1970s left his wife and three children and a comfortable life in order to honor Shiva. He embarked on the path of austerity with a single possession: a trident known as a *trisul*, which in Hinduism is used by Shiva to destroy human ignorance.

His years as a beggar were not sufficient for Bharati to feel he had pleased Shiva, so he decided to raise his arm to the heavens to ask for peace.

For nearly fifty years, he kept his arm raised as if touching the sky, tolerating the pain, the calcification of his bones, and the atrophy of his muscles. He lost the use of his arm and all feeling in it, but he maintained the gesture and became a living myth.

Neither Pleasure nor Pain Makes Us Slaves

Without reaching the extremes of Amar Bharati, the sadhus sometimes resolve to overcome the yoke of suffering with acts of extreme penance such as burying themselves in the ground, driving spikes through their tongues, sleeping while standing on just one leg, walking over hot coals, or setting out on a "rolling" pilgrimage across great distances.

This resistance to pain, along with the practice of meditation and fasting and sometimes a vow of silence, is common among the different orders of sadhus. Their asceticism is expressed according to the sect they belong to. Let's look at the three most representative sects:

1. The Naga sadhus, originally warriors who contained the Muslim invasions in the twelfth century, wear as their only garment the ashes of bodies cremated in purification. They are hermits who usually live isolated lives in the Himalayas, though they traverse great distances to participate in large gatherings of pilgrims.

2. The Aghori sadhus embrace the most extreme and radical rituals. They live near crematoriums, where they participate in postmortem ceremonies. To show that death is part of life, they sometimes eat the unincinerated flesh of the dead or drink from a human skull. Occasionally, they even eat their own feces. Though most orthodox Hindus reject their practices, the Aghori sadhus are especially revered in rural areas.

3. The Dandi sadhus, so called because of the bamboo staff, or *danda*, they always carry, are scholars of the sacred texts who devote themselves to meditation.

The process of joining one of these three sects can vary, but every sadhu will need a guru to accompany him and show him the value of renunciation.

TEACHERS, MENTORS, GURUS

At some point in our lives, we all need a guide. In India, this role is performed by a guru, or spiritual guide.

Just as the sadhus receive their initiation from a teacher, many well-known people have benefited from a mentor figure who has shown them the steps to follow and nurtured their confidence.

Mother Teresa developed a strong connection to Father Michael van der Peet, who encouraged her to devote her life to the needy. Facebook founder Mark Zuckerberg sought help from another famous technology guru, Apple founder Steve Jobs. Oprah Winfrey counted the poet and artist Maya Angelou as her mentor, and Quincy Jones received guidance from none other than Ray Charles.

Having a first-rate guide was crucial in order for all these people to reach great heights and give the best of themselves. And you? Do you have a mentor who can steer you toward where you want to go?

Life Is a Pilgrimage

Historians ascribe the expansion of Hinduism to the sadhus. Thanks to their devotion to pilgrimage—the central thread of their lives—their faith has left a major mark on Southeast Asia.

We find the highest number of sadhus in the Sapta Puri, India's holy places—in Rishikesh, where they cultivate control of the body and mind by practicing yoga, as well as in other locations, especially Varanasi, where the Ganges receives those who wish to be freed from suffering.

These cities mark their route, since the sacred rivers of the Ganges, Yamuna, and Saraswati flow through them. In the major pilgrims' gathering of Kumbh Mela, or Kumbha Mela, a festival attended by millions, the sadhu sing to Mother Ganges and hold processions lasting for weeks, displaying their rituals and their unmistakable appearance.

The influence of the sadhus transcends the Asian continent. Between 1845 and 1917, more than thirty-five thousand immigrated to Jamaica, where they pioneered the planting of ganja (marijuana), a name inspired by the River Ganges, the goddess Kali, and the god Shiva.

Wearing hair in dreadlocks, too, had an influence on Rastafarian culture. In Hindi, *rasta* means "path" or "way." Music legend Bob Marley helped to make dreadlocks—a symbol of the sadhus—known all over the world.

HE WITH THE LONG HAIR

"He with the long hair endures fire, he with the long hair endures poison, he with the long hair endures both worlds. They say he with the long hair looks straight at the sky, they say he with the long hair is himself that light . . . we are mortals, they only gaze at our bodies . . . For him, the Lord of life has whipped and beaten he who is inflexible, when he with the long hair, in the company of Rudra, drank from the cup of poison."

—FROM THE "KESIN HYMN" OF THE *RIG VEDA*

The Mountain of Existence

What can we learn from the sadhus about the art of happiness?

We can learn to give up the things we do not truly need. This will allow us to tread lightly on our planet and diminish the wear and tear of life.

The psychologist and writer Joan Garriga provides a striking explanation of this, using a mountain as a metaphor for life.

In the first half of our lives, we climb the mountain with the desire to make gains. We accumulate knowledge, experiences, friendships, loves, professional or intellectual milestones, all kinds of possessions. . . . Then, at the midpoint of our life's journey, we reach the top of the mountain and shout, "Here I am! Here's everything I have achieved!" and we enjoy the view of the world from our lookout point.

Yet once we have reached the top, we must go down the other side of the mountain. We are weary from the climb, and our dwindling strength will continue to fade as we make the descent. Having passed the midpoint of life, the wise person ceases to accumulate things in this second part of the journey and starts letting them go. We free ourselves from the useless items taking up space and weighing us down. We begin to need less and less, and we prioritize traveling light, until at the end of our descent, we let go of all we have left—life itself.

Joan Garriga observes the sadness of people who go down the mountain with a spirit of accumulation. Rather than simplifying their lives and keeping only the essentials, valuing time above all else, they persist in their desire to conquer, to prove themselves, filling their schedules and demanding rewards. They can neither delegate nor let go.

THE WAY OF THE SADHU

These are the people who should learn from the wisdom of the sadhus.

What Can You Live Without?

There is a German comedy film in which two friends, as a result of a bet, decide to give up everything they have. They spend a hundred days naked between four walls, and each day they can reintroduce one of the things they have parted with. This is how they will find out what they really need.

This film made us think of a self-help classic published in 1994: *Simplify Your Life*, which Elaine St. James wrote after fifteen years of grueling work as a real estate agent.

Overwhelmed by her packed schedule and a constantly expanding to-do list, St. James went on a weekend retreat to rethink her life. While there, she made a list of all the things she could do to reduce the complexity of her day-to-day life. Among them:

- Moving to a part of the country where she really wanted to live; to a smaller house that would allow her to save money and time on its upkeep

THE FOUR-WAY PATH

- Changing careers in favor of an activity she liked much more, even if it meant she would have less earning power
- Selling the "damn boat" that she didn't use and that was causing her such a headache
- Radically reducing her need for possessions and services
- Rethinking her dietary and shopping habits

To conclude this chapter, we recommend doing the Elaine St. James exercise. You don't need to be a sadhu to streamline your life. In fact, you don't even need to go on a weekend retreat.

Set aside an hour just for you. Take yourself on a date to a café or a park and make a list of the following in your notebook:

- All the material objects you can live without—you can sell them or give them away to free up time and space
- Pointless or unnecessary expenses
- Meetings and engagements you attend but that don't really appeal to you; relationships you maintain only out of inertia

- Daily habits—watching TV, aimless scrolling online, etc.—that you do not choose in a completely conscious way; all the inessential things that you do on autopilot

Once you have identified all the things you can live without, use the characters in that German film as inspiration and eliminate from your life one thing on your list.

Do this for one hundred days and see how much it lightens your load. Welcome to the path of the sadhu!

The Ashram

Growing in Community

In our research in the north of Okinawa that inspired the books that brought us here, we discovered that one of the keys to longevity is maintaining a strong circle of friends—a spiritual family. The moais we visited in Ogimi, where the elderly celebrate birthdays, play games, and provide mutual support—including financial support thanks to a communal fund—are one of the reasons people live longer and enjoy a superior quality of life in that part of the world. In fact, *moai* can be translated as "gathering with a common purpose."

A strong social circle favors longevity and also happiness. As the poet John Donne wrote in the seventeenth century, "No man is an island." We need others in order to feel mentally and spiritually healthy.

Those we spend time with have a significant impact on our well-being. If we choose them wisely, we will feel fortified in difficult times, comforted in times of sadness, and stimulated to carry out our ideas and projects.

In India there is a tradition of ashrams, spiritual communities that gather around a teacher or specific faith. These are the subject of this chapter. Just as surrounding yourself with the right people will nourish your greatest virtues, choosing the wrong ashram might drag you down instead of raising you up.

Toiling Toward

Spiritual practice, community routine, and the search for mental peace are some of the goals of ashrams. They are open to anyone wanting to learn about meditation and yoga and are an oasis for inner growth and for observing how we would like to live.

Their doors are open both to sadhus making their pilgrimages from one monastery to another and to locals, regardless of caste. Travelers seeking distance from the noise of the world to contemplate what makes them happy in a simple setting are also welcome. And this happiness, whether

you are Buddhist, Hindu, or neither, can be found only inside you.

Ashrams date back to ancient times, when they were
usually located outside the cities, in a regenerative natural
setting. Havens of tranquility, they still offer accommodations, teachings, and a pause in the journey for explorers of
the soul today.

Some accept volunteers who assist with the upkeep of the
space and its services. Others open their arms unconditionally and offer a retreat for people to rediscover themselves.

We can see the philosophy of the ashram in the word's
Sanskrit etymology—it means "religious exertion." In the
Hindu tradition, the ashram is a place for the study of Vedic
texts and the practice of yoga and meditation. Spiritual
progress toward the fourth purushartha (*moksha*, or spiritual liberation) is cultivated through these activities and
through strict self-discipline applied to diet and schedule.

An essential aspect of the ashram is its function as a *gu-
rukul* or "house of the guru," where students live together
and receive inspiration from a teacher or spiritual guide.

In India there are spiritual communities inspired by the
teachings of any number of guides, among them the con-
troversial Rajneesh (later called Osho); Mirra Alfassa, "the
Mother," who collaborated with Sri Aurobindo and who the

experimental township Auroville; Ramakrishna; Ramana Maharshi; Jiddu Krishnamurti; and the Amma, "the hugging saint," with her long lines to receive an embrace.

THE MIND IS MADE UP OF FOOD (AND THE HAPPIEST FOOD IS INDIAN)

Among the habits encouraged in an ashram is that of maintaining a light and balanced diet that favors the utmost concentration and mental clarity, as we can read in the *Chandogya Upanishad*:

Food, when eaten, becomes divided into three parts: That which is its grossest ingredient becomes the fecal matter. Its middling part becomes flesh, and its subtlest part becomes the mind. Dear boy, of the curd that is being churned, that which is the subtlest part rises upwards, and becomes clarified butter. In the same way, dear boy, of the food that is being eaten, that which is the subtlest part rises upwards, and becomes the Mind. Hence, dear boy, mind is made up of food.

According to a study by the German online food delivery platform Lieferando, it is Indian food that makes us feel the happiest, with curry increasing the happiness of the eater by 83 percent.

The spices used in the preparation of curry might be responsible, especially turmeric, which, according to a study by UCLA, improves the mood of those who eat it.

Nourishing Calm

Most ashrams in India base their diets on guidelines inspired by the precepts of Ayurveda. Even if we're not on a retreat at a spiritual center, we can still apply these rules for a healthy body, mind, and spirit in our own home:

- Eat fresh foods that have not been prepared more than three hours before.
- Remove processed foods from your diet, as well as caffeine, soda, sugar, and frozen, fried, and packaged foods.
- Dairy and fruit should never be combined, nor should more than 100 milliliters of water be drunk before their consumption.
- We should maintain a regular eating schedule. A digestive system requires a fixed temporal guide for the microbiota to work optimally.

- Before eating, we should stimulate our gastric juices with a little ginger.
- To taste our food better, we should concentrate on it exclusively. To this end, we should eat slowly and silently, as is done at a mindfulness retreat. Purists recommend chewing each mouthful thirty-two times to improve digestion, mouthful after mouthful.
- We should avoid distractions like reading or conversation while we eat.

When we eat, we should be aware that what feeds us is energy that comes from the Earth and the Universe. It is therefore a gift from God.

Eating in a conscious and healthy way, whether at an ashram or at home, will provide us with energy and physical and mental wellness. It is a fundamental part of the way to happiness.

The Benefits of a Retreat

Why are there so many people who need to abandon their daily whirlwind and put a halt to their mind's incessant ruminations? The causes are as varied as the kinds of people who decide to dive into this experience, but these are the most common motives for going on a retreat:

- To connect with our inner selves and get to know ourselves better; to have the space and silence to observe ourselves and accept change without fear
- To learn to be patient and humble through meditation or any other spiritual practice
- To learn to be generous, setting aside individualism and selfishness, while feeling that we are part of something larger than ourselves
- To purge our body and mind of toxic elements; to rest from the noise of the world and recharge our batteries for the challenges coming our way
- To connect with a teacher or guide who can shed new light on the path we have taken, and with other pilgrims who might be living through a similar moment. Even on silent retreats, the presence of other people is inspiring and makes our quest easier.

Daily life at an ashram unfolds in a space with dormitories that are usually shared; a communal dining room; rooms for meditation, yoga, and reading; and a garden.

Though silence is compulsory only if we participate in a

vipassana retreat or similar, we will be asked to speak in a low voice and to wear comfortable, loose-fitting, and modest clothes (they should not reveal arms, legs, or torsos), such as long dresses, *punjabi* suits, *dhotis*, and long shirts.

Physical contact is restricted—in most monasteries, celibacy is required. Smoking, drinking alcohol, and taking drugs are also prohibited.

The day follows a timetable from when we get up with the sunrise until we retire when night falls. Each day includes the *satsang*—a time for meditation, chanting mantras, and reading—yoga sessions, and light meals.

The ashram lifestyle is intentionally austere. Going back to basics allows us to detect what we do not need so we can glimpse the foundations of our happiness.

DISCONNECTION AND RECONNECTION: *EAT, PRAY, LOVE*

To write the section dedicated to spirituality in her bestselling memoir *Eat, Pray, Love*, Elizabeth Gilbert spent a period at an ashram in India. In Italy she learned the rituals and emotions associated with food, and in Bali she focused on the body and feeling love, but it was at the Ganeshpuri ashram—where it is speculated that she stayed—that she experienced spiritual cleansing and reconnection.

The Beatles' Spiritual Refuge

For Maharishi Mahesh, the guru who initiated the Beatles into meditation, happiness is the only true success. In 1968, members of the most famous band of all time traveled with their partners and other family members to Rishikesh, the sacred city on the shores of the Ganges known as the yoga capital, where some of the most renowned ashrams in India are located.

The Beatle who was the most passionate about these spiritual discoveries was George Harrison, who justified his disappearance from the world as being necessary for recovering life's meaning. After years of fame and fortune, he felt he was lacking true love and peace.

George's fascination caught on with the whole band, and together they went on a retreat to the Chaurasi Kutia ashram, named by Maharishi Mahesh, the founder of the Transcendental Meditation technique. There, they would write their iconic "White Album."

In the nineties, the ashram was abandoned, and only recently did it reopen to visitors, mostly Beatles fans who walk reverently through the ruined buildings covered in moss and spiderwebs.

The songs written here include "Dear Prudence," which invited the actress Mia Farrow's sister to emerge from her seclusion at the ashram. Prudence would later become a Transcendental Meditation teacher.

Another song inspired by the period at Rishikesh is "I'm So Tired," which describes John Lennon's mood after a time of withdrawal, when he was unable to drink alcohol or take drugs. It wasn't easy for the Fab Four to say no to life's pleasures.

Three Lessons for Personal Happiness

You might never go on a retreat to an ashram or a monastery. And even if you do, a retreat is a vacation from the everyday life to which you will have to return.

So how can we bring the serenity and clarity of a spiritual break to our daily lives?

Three practical methods occur to us:

1. *Create your own oasis at home.* This can be a small sacred space where you can relax. A nook with a rug, some cushions, and a table. Or your favorite armchair. If you have a house, it can be a room you can retreat to, in every sense of the word, without anyone bothering you. An oasis doesn't even have to be a physical space if you don't have access to a peaceful corner. It can be a certain hour you reserve every day for self-care with no external distractions: you could meditate, read, listen to music, or simply think. You can keep a notebook handy to write down any thoughts that occur to you.

2. *Adopt the good habits of a monastery.* The whirlwind of our day-to-day life does not allow us to live as if we are at a vipassana retreat, but we can bring into our lives some of the practices that have benefited us, such as a conscious and healthy diet, or enough hours dedicated to silence and rest. You can decide which aspects of monastic living you bring into your daily life.

3. *Take care of your circle.* Like the moai, an ashram is—or ought to be—a group of people working toward

a common goal. It is therefore important to make good decisions about where we want to belong and whom we want to be with. Emotional contagion means that we end up resembling the people we often see. This is why it is so important to examine the community we have created around us. Do we share the same basic principles? Do they add value to our life or subtract it? Do they help or hinder our spiritual growth? In the end, the quality of our circle will determine the quality of our life.

Teachers in Our Time

In the first section of this book, we devoted a chapter to the old teachers of India, who were ahead of their time and asked questions that are highly relevant today. In the modern era, in addition to Rabindranath Tagore, the first non-European to win the Nobel Prize in Literature, and twentieth-century thinkers such as Jiddu Krishnamurti, it is the technology and business sphere that has more and more Indian gurus who are called upon to be leaders.

We became aware of this new wave of talent when we visited India just before the pandemic.

On our literary tour of India, we had the good fortune to share a stage with a number of influential Indians. To give his version of ikigai, a Mumbai entrepreneur described a personal experience that we like to recount, and that we shared with readers of the magazine *CuerpoMente* (*BodyMind*).

According to this man, his business had been growing

for some time, until his firm became a multinational. Before he left on a trip to New York, where he would be signing one of the most fruitful contracts of his life, his mother gave him a small envelope.

"What is this, Mother?" he asked her.

"Don't open it yet," she replied. "It's a gift for the important trip you're about to make."

Intrigued, he put the envelope in his wallet. As soon as he landed in New York and stepped off the plane, he took it out and opened it. Inside was a piece of paper with a single word written in his mother's hand: "ENOUGH."

In a state of shock, he immediately called his mother and asked her to explain the meaning of the gift.

"Calm down, my son. If you don't understand on your way there, you'll understand on your way back."

Increasingly disconcerted, he put the envelope away and decided to pour himself into the negotiation awaiting him in the city that never sleeps.

A couple of days later, he caught his flight back to Mumbai. Despite traveling in first class with the best possible service, as soon as the plane took off, he felt utterly exhausted. It wasn't just physical and mental. After the high he'd felt from the contract he had signed, an immense existential fatigue had taken hold of him.

As his plane pierced the clouds, he thought deep down that the life that had seemed so exciting and was so impressive to others bored him. It had stopped making sense.

Just then he remembered his mother's envelope and her oracular words: "If you don't understand on your way there, you'll understand on your way back." When he held the word "ENOUGH" before his eyes, it gained a new meaning.

It had all been fine until then—it had even been enjoyable—but he had no desire to remain on that path. He could double his wealth, even multiply it by ten, but the void he felt inside would be the same or worse.

Once he was back in his city, he made a radical decision. He would leave the business world behind and devote himself to a mission that had been knocking at the door of his conscience for a long time, though he had not wanted to acknowledge it: providing a high-quality education to the most disadvantaged students.

When the businessman shifted his attention to the new task that lay before him, he felt a youthful energy coursing through his body again. He began to plan out how to invest his resources to train teachers and professors who would share their knowledge with collectives who lacked access to that level of education.

He soon had an ambitious program, a team of collaborators, a calendar, and medium- and long-term goals. The entrepreneur was now in his prime. Having been lost for years, he had found the meaning of his life, his ikigai. He ended his captivating speech with these words:

"I can now say that I am happy. I feel fulfilled and useful to society. And I'll tell you one last secret. Today, everyone wants to be everywhere, to communicate with everyone, to multiply their presence. There is an illusion that this is success, but I tell you, this is completely wrong. Success is achieved by the opposite route: by closing doors. Only if you close the door to everything inessential will you be able to focus on what is really important and be a successful human being."

The Impossible Mathematician: Srinivasa Ramanujan

There are geniuses who close doors to devote themselves to their ikigai, and other geniuses who open doors that nobody knew were there.

Before visiting a few current technology leaders, let's go back to 1887 and look at a unique case in the world of science. Srinivasa Ramanujan was born in the district of Erode, in Tamil Nadu. He would die at the tender age of thirty-two. Yet despite living such a short life, he is considered one of the greatest mathematicians in history.

What makes his case extraordinary is that he was a complete autodidact from childhood, using only books and his intuition.

Such was his genius that during a conversation from his hospital bed, he conceived an idea that would be an entirely new contribution to mathematics, which today is known as taxicab or Hardy-Ramanujan numbers.

This is how his mentor G. H. Hardy, from the London Mathematical Society, tells the story: "I remember once going to see him when he was lying ill at Putney. I had ridden in taxicab number 1729 and remarked that the number seemed to me rather a dull one, and that I hoped it was not an unfavorable omen. 'No,' he replied, 'it is a very interesting number; it is the smallest number expressible as the sum of two cubes in two different ways.'"

But let's go back to when Ramanujan was an unknown young man in India. With no formal studies, how did he manage to be accepted by this renowned professor at Cambridge University?

Ramanujan was born into a poor family. His father was an assistant in a clothing store and his mother a housewife. When he was eleven years old, a book of trigonometry by an English mathematician fell into his hands. Reading and studying this book would change his life.

After two years of studying it, he began to elaborate his own theorems based on the knowledge he was acquiring. At fourteen, Ramanujan's school performance was already outstanding, and he finished his math exams in half the allotted time, though he was less brilliant in other subjects.

In fact, upon completing his secondary education, he tried to continue his studies in college, but he failed nearly all his subjects except mathematics. This forced him to leave college, but he continued to persevere independently with his favorite subject. His obsession with numbers led to a life of extreme poverty.

He got a job as an accountant in Madras (now Chennai) with the modest monthly salary of thirty rupees. His skill with numbers allowed him to finish his workday early and devote the rest of his time to his mathematical research.

With the help of some English-speaking friends, he began writing letters to eminent mathematicians in the United Kingdom, since in those days India was a British colony. His first attempts to demonstrate his theories were rejected for lack of rigor, and in other cases he seemed like a fraud—the mathematical results he showed on the pages he sent with his letters were so exceptional that it was hard to believe they had been arrived at by a young man.

However, Ramanujan was not discouraged. When one of his letters reached G. H. Hardy, the professor recognized his talent.

Ramanujan's letter was nine pages long. This is how it began:

Dear Sir,

I beg to introduce myself to you as a clerk in the Accounts Department of the Port Trust Office at Madras on a salary of only £20 per annum. I am now about 23 years of age. I have had no University education, but I have undergone the ordinary school course. After leaving school I have been employing the spare time at my disposal to work at Mathematics. I have not trodden through the conventional regular course which is followed in a University course, but I am striking out a new path for myself. I have made a special investigation of

divergent series in general and the results I get are termed
by the local mathematicians as "startling."

The rest of the letter is packed with mathematical discoveries, but he does not provide proofs. Despite this, the results he showed in the letter were so surprising that G. H. Hardy decided to invite him to London to work with him.

Ramanujan had to decline the invitation because his mother refused to let him go. Despite this, Hardy persisted, asking an English mathematician who taught in Madras to be Ramanujan's mentor and to try to convince him to come to London.

One day, Ramanujan's mother had a vivid dream in which the goddess Namagiri Thayar—a Hindu deity who was important in her family—appeared and told her "to stand no longer between her son and the fulfilment of his life's purpose." After receiving such a direct message, she decided to give her son permission to go to England.

Finally, in 1914, Ramanujan sailed to London. He worked alongside G. H. Hardy for several years and became a member of the London Mathematical Society and of the Royal Society, a society for the advancement of science that had counted Isaac Newton, Charles Darwin, and Albert Einstein among its members.

Diagnosed with tuberculosis, Ramanujan returned to Madras in 1919, and died in 1920 at only thirty-two.

One hundred years later, his legacy continues to contribute to the advancement of mathematics. To cite one example, in the 1990s, Andrew Wiles used Galois theory, based on congruences discovered by Ramanujan, to prove Fermat's last theorem.

Lessons in Brilliance from Ramanujan

Ramanujan's unusual talent makes us think of those young Indians whom the Mumbai entrepreneur who decided to devote himself to educating the disadvantaged wants to bring out into the world so they can shine. There are several keys from the story of this young mathematician that we can apply to our daily lives.

- *Autodidacticism and independent study, so common in our era of YouTube tutorials, help you think outside the box and come up with different ideas.* Perhaps because he was not trained in academia, Ramanujan discovered many things in the field of mathematics that until then no one had even thought of. As the multifaceted artist Jean Cocteau put it, he did it because he did not know that it couldn't be done.

- *A book can change your life forever.* That volume of trigonometry that fell into Ramanujan's hands when he was a child lit the initial spark of his ikigai, or his life's purpose. What book is on your nightstand right now? What clues can it give you about your new life?

- *There is a genius inside you, waiting to be discovered.* What might have happened if Ramanujan had never had access to math books? Society is sometimes unjust and hard on those who are bad at almost everything but who have a great talent in one area. If you are a parent or teacher, or are in a position of influence, try to unearth the treasure that lies dormant inside those who may not know that they have a certain talent. And don't forget to do the same with yourself.

- *Always be humble.* Even though he knew he was excellent at mathematics, Ramanujan offered himself as a student to the best in his field and let himself be guided by them. No matter how great your talent, you should trust in those who know more than you or have experience that offers a perspective you lack.

- *Dare to make contact.* Don't worry about the fame of the person you admire. If they could be the right mentor for you, it is always worth a try. A letter, an email, or another kind of message to the right person or institution can change your life's direction forever. Don't lose heart if the first thing you receive is rejection. Sometimes you have to knock on the door several times, or knock on several doors, to be let in. The only certain thing is that if you don't try, everything will stay the same.

MESSAGE ON A SURFBOARD

During a talk in Valencia (Spain), we met a woman who told us about her son's remarkable adventure.

Passionate about water sports since he was a child, he managed to get a job with the best water-sports store in London. The business served resorts and clubs all over the world and counted Virgin founder Richard Branson among its select clientele. Branson was living on Necker Island, a private island with luxury accommodations for twenty-eight people, where he had hosted Barack and Michelle Obama at the end of Barack Obama's exhausting two terms as president. Google cofounder Larry Page also got married on Necker Island.

Knowing these stories, the young man greatly admired Branson and dreamed of working as a water-sports instructor on his private island. While preparing to ship an order to Branson from the water-sports store, he decided to hide a letter to the English entrepreneur on a surfboard. In the letter, he explained his enormous desire to work for him.

To his amazement, a few weeks later he received an email from Branson, offering to fly him to the island for an interview. He must have liked the boy's attitude, since one of the Virgin founder's maxims is, "If your dreams don't scare you, they are too small."

The young man from Valencia was hired as an instructor for the magnate and his illustrious visitors. He spent several years on the island, working closely with Branson, until he left to set out on a new adventure, working in the world's other resorts.

Satya Nadella, CEO of Microsoft

It is impossible to write about Indian tech leaders without considering the example of Satya Nadella.

Born in 1967, the son of a Sanskrit professor and an Indian bureaucrat, Nadella moved to the United States in 1988. He graduated from the University of Wisconsin–Milwaukee with a degree in computer science and began working for Microsoft in 1992. He was one of the first thirty Indian immigrants to hold a position at Microsoft.

Twenty-two years after arriving at Microsoft, at the age of forty-six, he was named CEO by Bill Gates and Steve Ballmer.

Since Nadella took the helm at Microsoft in 2014, the company's stock value has multiplied, and in 2022 it had the second-highest market capitalization after Apple.

Nadella and Microsoft's Ikigai

In the first email Nadella sent to all employees after being named CEO, he explained the leitmotif, or guiding principle, of his life. He also clearly detailed the company's general raison d'être. Although he did not use the word *ikigai*, he clearly defined both his personal ikigai and that of the company in general, as well as that of all its employees.

He began the email by explaining his personal purpose: "I fundamentally believe that if you are not learning new things, you stop doing great and useful things. So family, curiosity, and hunger for knowledge all define me."

The email went on to establish the purpose of Microsoft:

"To paraphrase a quote from Oscar Wilde—we need to believe in the impossible and remove the improbable. This starts with clarity of purpose and sense of mission that will lead us to imagine the impossible and deliver it."

He ended by emphasizing the importance of everyone finding purpose in what they do every day:

"Finally, I truly believe that each of us must find meaning in our work. The best work happens when you know that it's not just work, but something that will improve other people's lives."

In this paragraph of his first email, where he emphasized the importance of "improving other people's lives," he made a clear allusion to the fourth circle of ikigai: "what the world needs."

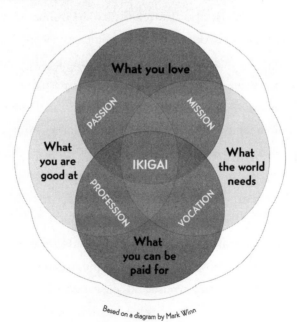

Based on a diagram by Mark Winn

The Two Necessary Conditions
for Being Hired at Microsoft

When Nadella took the reins of the company, he established what has become known internally as "Nadella's Necessities." These are the two conditions that the CEO considers essential when it comes to choosing whom to hire.

1. *Does this person create clarity?*

   The worst thing that can happen to a team is having a member who, though highly intelligent and capable, only creates confusion with their contributions. The best candidates are always those who help to create clarity with their participation.

2. *Does this person create positive energy?*

   All of us are drawn to people whose presence energizes us. Likewise, it is never pleasant to work with people who wrap us in a cloud of negative energy. In any project, whether it is professional or personal, the best candidates are those who bring positive energy into our lives.

Ajay V. Bhatt: The Coinventor of the USB

Born in India, Ajay V. Bhatt began working at Intel in 1990 after moving to the United States. In his more than twenty-five years at this multinational, he patented more than a hundred of his inventions. One of those is the USB plug that today is used on most electronic devices the world over.

It is fascinating to learn the everyday origin of this invention so often used today.

In the early 1990s, Bhatt's wife wanted to print some of her son's homework but was unable to do so because they did not have the right cable for their new computer. As he noticed his wife's frustration, Bhatt realized that it wasn't just her; everyone was frustrated with printer cables.

This was the spark that ignited Bhatt's creativity and drove him to lead the team that would define the original specifications of the USB: universal serial bus. The idea was to create a single cable that could be used with any kind of printer.

The product of this team's work was launched commercially in 1996, and with time it became the standard cable for connecting not just printers but also virtually any kind of electronic device.

Bhatt's determination to solve his family's everyday problem with a printer ended up creating the cable we now use to charge our cell phones.

Other Indian Tech Leaders

Since Ramanujan's spontaneous genius, India's influence in mathematics and computer programming has become so extensive that it could fill a whole book. Shantanu Narayen has been CEO of Adobe since 2007, after many years of working for Apple. Ajay Singh Banga was the CEO of Mastercard until recently and as of 2023 heads the World Bank, and Rajeev Suri has been CEO of Nokia since 2014.

We will highlight just a couple more people to complete this chapter about tech gurus.

- **Arvind Krishna: CEO of IBM.** Born in India, he studied at the Kanpur Institute of Technology before moving to the United States. In 1990 he began working at IBM, and after many years at IBM Research, where he created multiple patents, he became the first senior vice president and later CEO and president of the company.

- **Sundar Pichai: CEO of Google and Alphabet.** Pichai was born in Madras and moved to the United States to study at Stanford University. His first job after graduating was as a materials engineer, and he began working at Google in 2004. After just eleven years at the multinational, in 2015 he was appointed CEO. *Time* magazine has selected him twice as one of the world's hundred most influential people.

Jugaad

The people featured in this chapter have a special ability to solve problems, finding new solutions where others see only barriers. What is their secret?

There is an essential word that can provide an answer.

In our quest to discover the secrets of Indian culture, we were struck by the concept of *jugaad*, or *jugaar*. This colloquial Hindi term refers to the creative solutions we arrive at with minimal resources, often simply with whatever we have on hand at the time.

answering the question: What is a quick solution that I can adopt today?

Once we have the jugaad solution, or a hack that works halfway, we will feel more confident and able to move forward.

The jugaad philosophy can be applied to numerous areas of life. For example, to write a song, we can start with a simple tune or by composing four chords; to write a blog article, we can begin with a draft; for a new professional project, we can start with one or two ideas and progress from there.

The key is to get going and be practical. As the aphorism goes, "The perfect is the enemy of the good." Japanese therapist Shoma Morita added, "Be the best imperfect person you can be."

OM, the
Sacred Syllable

O M, or AUM, as it is sometimes transcribed, represents the sound of the Universe, and is therefore all-encompassing. In terms of modern astrophysics, OM can be associated with the big bang, which expands into infinity and later contracts: divine respiration.

At the same time, it points to our own breath, which connects us to life and emanates words, love, and vibrations that influence others. As the Indian spiritual teacher Amit Ray explains, what is important is not how long we live or how much money we make or whether we are famous. What remains is the positive vibration we have produced during our passage through this life.

There are more than ten possible translations of the sacred syllable, one of which is "Welcome to the divine."

The Whole Universe

As an element that symbolizes the Creator, Brahma, and as the source of the Universe, OM, also known as the OM syllable or *omkara*, is the most powerful sound in dharmic religions like Hinduism and Buddhism.

Because OM is understood as that which unifies body and spirit, the vibration where all other sounds are born, no mystical chant can be without it.

Such is the strength of OM that many spiritual teachers believe its vibration erases human errors and cleanses karma, clearing the path to spiritual liberation, as meditation expert Banani Ray explains.

For his part, the great guru Paramahansa Yogananda maintains that past, present, and future, along with all states of consciousness, travel through OM to finally reach the peace of silence.

In India, the chant is repeated three times to evoke the three deities who make up the Universe: Brahma, Vishnu, and Shiva. This trinity and the concept of creative sound can also be found in other religions, which utter "amen," "amin," or "hum" to confirm their faith in the sacred.

OM

A POPULAR TATTOO IS A SOUND

OM, or AUM, is visually expressed as a symbol made up of five parts: two of the strokes form a "3," which is completed by a third semicircular stroke to the right and a dot and a stroke above the lower figure, on top of the "3."

This symbol is a favorite tattoo of many famous actors and musicians. When they ink an OM symbol onto their skin, they invoke the states of consciousness:

- The lower stroke of the 3 represents *wakefulness* or *the awakened mind*, when our senses perceive everything.
- The upper stroke represents a *middle state between wakefulness and sleep*, when the mind remains active.
- The sleeping mind, located in the semicircular stroke, is *deep sleep* and zero mental perception, the third state of consciousness.
- The dot, the fourth state of consciousness, represents *mental peace, stillness, and happiness*. This is the state achieved with meditation, where OM is silence and disconnection.
- Finally, the horizontal stroke below the dot is *ignorance*, which prevents us from reaching the joy of the silent OM. This is attachment, suffering, and the illusion, or *maya*, caused by the mind.

For the force of the king of mantras to come to life, the three sounds must be intoned correctly:

- A, cosmic creativity, is pronounced briefly, and is the highest-pitched tone during meditation.
- U, balance, is sustained for longer and in a medium tone.
- M, dissolution, returns us to the beginning of the universal cycle, in a deep tone, like a hum.

Mantras: Protectors of the Mind

In Sanskrit, *mantra* is the combination of the terms *manas* (protection) and *tram* (mind). Mantras are repeated and act as a personal balm intended to care for and cultivate the soul and achieve liberation.

The act of making our voice resonate with a mantra regenerates us. It's like meeting Buddha or the *bodhisattva* himself, Tibetan monks say.

Just as a fence protects a cultivated field from being trampled by animals, a mantra protects the mind from temptation.

As we will see in the second part of this book, in the frameworks of both Hinduism and Buddhism, mantras are steeped in faith, whether in the divine or in the search for nirvana. Since mantras are not conceptual, their benefits for the spirit are pure; they do not pass through thought.

In mantras, OM is the foundational syllable, the seed from which prayer and concentration emerge. The mystical chant of OM allows us to look inside ourselves and focus. This is the *dharani*, which in Sanskrit describes a state of peace and happiness.

As the myths of the Puranas—the sacred texts that came after the Vedas—tell us, OM brings together all manifestations of the act of creation, expressed as the sound of the Universe, shaping it all like a mother giving birth.

When OM is pronounced, the sound and the air make the body and mind vibrate.

The best-known mantra in Buddhism is OM MANI PADME HUM. Its six syllables allude to the bodhisattva of compassion, called Avalokiteshvara in Sanskrit and Chenrezig in Tibetan. This mantra of "the jewel in the lotus"—this is its literal meaning—expresses the feeling of purification derived from passing through the six kingdoms of Buddhist existence: happiness (OM) crushes pride; patience (MA) puts a stop to envy; discipline (NI) placates passion; wisdom (PAD) counteracts stupidity; generosity (ME) erases the desire for possessions; and diligence (HUM) does away with violence and hatred.

THE JEDI MANTRA

Fans of Star Wars may be familiar with the mantra that director George Lucas, who has been influenced by Buddhism, dreamed up for the saga. In the world of Star Wars, the meditations of the Jedi include the mantra OM MANI PADME HUM.

The Jedi evoke the idea of living with integrity, as the Buddhist Noble Eightfold Path requires. When Anakin Skywalker loses his purity and compassion by fearing death, he strays from the path and becomes Darth Vader.

Many die-hard fans of the Star Wars movies have turned for inner peace to the meditative practices inspired by the teachings and thoughts voiced by characters like Luke Skywalker and in particular Yoda, who guides the Jedi in their liberation from fear, anger, and uncontrolled desire.

These days, the Jedi Church has an immense number of followers all over the world.

The Joy of Meditation

There are festivals and tests documenting the ability to chant an OM for hours, but this kind of practice is detached from the true introspection to which the sacred syllable leads.

The regenerative, creative sound is not a remedy but rather a means of achieving the highest state of consciousness.

Even so, science has focused on the effects that this vocal practice has on the brain. A pilot study of the experience of OM chanting showed that the vibration of the voice deactivates the limbic system, resulting in the relaxation of the brain's amygdala and hippocampus, which are responsible for depression and anxiety when they react, for example, to stress.

For this reason, meditation while chanting OM is a significant neuroregulatory tool.

The Healing Power of Sound

OM is not the only healing sound to come from Asia. Since the year 480 BC, Eastern medicine has included the "voice" of Tibetan singing bowls. Made from an alloy of seven metals associated with the celestial bodies (lead: Saturn; gold: Sun; silver: Moon; copper: Venus; iron: Mars; mercury: Mercury; tin: Jupiter), they vibrate to the note of the OM mantra to strengthen concentration.

Traditional Chinese medicine also recommends the technique of the six healing sounds of Qigong. *Xu*, *he*, *hu*, *si*, *chui*, and *xi* resonate through the body's organs and in the emotions associated with them, with the purpose of reestablishing energetic balance.

Many yoga practitioners affirm that the OM mantra has benefits; among them:

- eliminating toxins from the body and maintaining hormonal and immune system balance
- helping to calm the emotions, since it helps focus and de-stress the mind
- improving and strengthening the vocal cords and breathing
- leading to a state of well-being

According to the Hindu tradition, to enjoy the benefits of OM, one should pronounce the sacred syllable 108 times. Other traditions, however, maintain that it is enough to repeat it between ten and twenty times to be filled with serenity.

Sometimes, a single OM pronounced at the right moment can return us to our lost state of peace.

II

THE PHILOSOPHY OF HAPPINESS

....

The Indian Paths to Personal Fulfillment

The Power of Self-Exploration

I n 1948, the German philosopher Karl Jaspers coined the term *Axial Age* to describe a period in the history of humanity when thinkers with no mutual contact had similar ideas and reached similar conclusions.

The golden age of Greek philosophy coincided with the appearance of thinkers such as Lao-tzu and Confucius in China and of the Buddha in India, among other spiritual guides. If we compare their teachings, we can identify some amazing coincidences.

In his book *The Origin and Goal of History*, Jaspers points out that the focus of these philosophers of the Axial Age was twofold: ethics of community well-being on the one hand and self-knowledge on the other.

Religious historian Karen Armstrong addresses this fascinating point of encounter in *The Great Transformation*, in which she claims that human beings have never surpassed the wisdom of those masters in Greece, China, and India.

The fact that we continue to study them in our daily lives is proof of this.

Armstrong establishes in her book some common characteristics of these guides from the Axial Age:

1. Rather than taking old beliefs as given, they begin to question everything.
2. Repeated ritual is replaced with reflection. Faith is replaced with exploration.
3. Philosophers appear in public and dare to dissent from any idea.

Armstrong points out that most of these thinkers appeared at moments of great crisis or profound change in their society, as is the case in our times. This caused them to reach the conclusion that humanity will be saved only by seeking greater self-knowledge and focusing on the common good, even if this is simply because we are all in the same boat.

Pilgrimage Mile Zero

Before setting out on a pilgrimage, as the pilgrim plans the different stages and the number of miles to cover each day, she must be familiar with her strengths and weaknesses. The path is different for an athletic person accustomed to sustained physical exertion than for someone less fit.

The journey's success will depend on the walker's self-knowledge. This is the case with any search we undertake in our lives, including for our own happiness.

Since we published *Ikigai*, we have done thousands of interviews, presentations, and talks in numerous countries. One question we are asked very often is: Where should you begin when you don't know your life's purpose?

We always explain that there is a prerequisite: knowing yourself. If you do not know who you are, having a purpose is useless, since it is intimately linked to your values and priorities in life. That is where you must begin.

THE TREASURE OF TREASURES

As Pausanias wrote in the second century AD, a now famous inscription could be seen at the entrance to the Temple of Apollo in Delphi, where hundreds of pilgrims went to consult the oracle on their future: "Know thyself."

Less known is the longer inscription found by visitors in the room of the Sybils, the women trained since childhood to reveal the messages of the oracles: "Know thyself."

The Question

We will talk about Ramana Maharshi several times in this second part of the book, since this wise man acted as a hinge between the past and the present of Advaita, a spiritual path we will get to know later.

For now, it is enough to know that he was born in 1879 in a small village in the south of India and that after his father's death, when he was twelve years old, he was sent to live with his uncle in the city of Madurai.

He would become a guru venerated all over India and the West. Thousands came to his ashram from all over the world in search of a spiritual awakening. He recommended that all of them practice *atma vichara*, which can be translated as "self-inquiry."

To do this, you just need to enter into a dialogue with yourself, beginning by asking, *Who am I?* An apparently simple question, but one that is difficult to answer. For this reason,

Ramana Maharshi recommended asking this question over and over until we reach the depths of ourselves.

Let's imagine that we are in the presence of this great teacher and that he can hear and comment on our answers to the question: *Who am I?*

H: I'm Héctor.

F: I'm Francesc.

RM: No, those are just your names. Who are you?

F: I'm a linguist, but I work as a writer and speaker.

H: I'm a computer engineer, and I combine that with writing, which is my passion.

RM: You haven't answered the question! That is your training, your profession, your work. . . . You must give an answer to something much more important and essential than that. Ask yourselves again: Who am I?

This is where the true challenge of self-exploration begins. If *who I am* has nothing to do with my name or the family I was born into, or my studies, hobbies, or work, or my possessions, then *who am I?*

To answer the question, we can draw upon the quote: "You only truly possess that which you cannot lose in a shipwreck." And what is that which you cannot lose in a shipwreck?

We have some ideas, but we don't want to influence you. We invite you to find a few quiet moments so you can ask yourself these life-changing questions.

The Four Detachments

....

It is said that many Japanese people go through three religions during their lives. They are born as Shintoists, adopting the country's ancestral spiritual practice; they are married as Christians, perhaps because they replicate the weddings they have seen in Hollywood movies; and they die as Buddhists, practicing detachment.

We are going to take a moment to consider Buddhism. It originated with an Indian prince, Siddhartha Gautama, who would become Buddha, which means "awakened one" or "enightened one." The religion is followed today by more than five hundred million people all over the world.

If we assume that happiness is our natural state, as we can see from babies' smiles, one way to recover it is to become less attached to everything that smothers it.

As if we're peeling the layers of an onion, each time we

free ourselves from an attachment, we come closer to the heart of happiness.

Detaching from the Material: Buddha on the Road

Siddhartha Gautama's spiritual apprenticeship began when he gave up all the comforts of his palace, where his father protected him from the world's troubles, to set out along the road as an ascetic.

Moving from the solid to the fluid, trading security for adventure, is a constant in the lives of all truth seekers.

What moved the young man born in Lumbini, today part of Nepal, is essentially no different from what drives the protagonists of Jack Kerouac's novel *On the Road* to wander across the United States and Mexico in search of experiences and wisdom. In the novel, Kerouac tells of the travels of a group of bohemians—several from wealthy backgrounds— between 1947 and 1950 as they search for the intricacies of existence, just like Siddhartha in his pursuit of answers to free himself from suffering.

KEROUAC'S SCROLL

On the Road, considered the masterpiece of the Beat Generation, was written in scarcely three weeks in the apartment that Kerouac shared with his second wife in Manhattan.

Instead of writing on sheets of paper, Kerouac used a long roll of paper, typing on it with neither margins nor paragraph breaks.

To shape his journeys of initiation into a novel, the only drug Kerouac used while writing was coffee. He seems to have started writing the book in French, the language of his parents, who came from Quebec, before switching to English.

To move forward with our spiritual search, we must cast off any attachment to material things, just like the sadhus, the pilgrims to whom we devoted a whole chapter. This doesn't necessarily mean being poor, like Siddhartha when he wandered half-naked and malnourished along the roads, but rather preventing material possessions from getting in the way of our happiness.

One example often given when we talk about this kind of attachment is a new car. A person falls in love with a brand-new model they have seen in commercials and ads. It is an expensive vehicle, so they hesitate and do lots of calculations before deciding to buy it on a four-year payment plan.

The day they leave the dealership with their shiny car, they are gripped by a euphoria that is not destined to last. After only a few days of taking to the roads, they find a scratch across the door. Maybe someone did this deliberately, or maybe it's just an accident, but in any case, the car is no longer new and flawless.

Something darkens in the owner's soul.

A few months later, the car will have a few little dents and dings. Now if they wanted to sell it, they would get only half what they paid, even if the body had suffered no damage at all. It is no longer new and each day it loses value, though the owner will keep making payments for the next several years.

The light that warmed their heart when they left the dealership has been extinguished, and now they simply feel sad and disappointed. That is attachment.

One of the insights the Buddha arrived at when he sat under the fig tree for seven days and seven nights is that seeking permanent satisfaction in impermanent things is a highway to unhappiness.

If the car owner had bought a twenty-year-old clunker

without having had to take out a loan, dents or scratches wouldn't have mattered. And they matter even less to the protagonists of *On the Road*, who jump from one bus to another with no possessions other than their longing to travel.

Does this mean that the fewer material possessions you have, the happier you'll be?

It would be simplistic to claim this is the case, but we are all familiar with the saying "The richest person is not the one who has the most, but the one who needs the least." Thinking that objects will bring permanent happiness when this can come only from inside, from intangible sources, is certainly a serious error in judgment.

The current rise of minimalism—"less is more"—is in keeping with this view. It is better to have three comfortable sweaters that we will wear hundreds of times than a closet full of clothes gathering dust. It is better to have one good friend than to deal with the clamor of a hundred acquaintances.

Once you have what you need to live peacefully, why complicate things?

THE MINIMALISTS

In 2015, Netflix premiered *The Minimalists: Less Is Now*, a documentary starring Ryan Nicodemus and Joshua Fields Millburn, who started the website theminimalists.com.

Friends since childhood, the two men had allowed themselves to be trapped by moneymaking fever and worked from dawn to dusk to make six-figure salaries, which was causing them an unhealthy amount of stress and anxiety and leading them to accumulate things they did not need. Nicodemus felt like he was filling his life with things.

Fields Millburn was the first to disconnect from this lifestyle. After quitting the job that was killing him, he left his blind consumption behind and began to recover his happiness. He felt like he was traveling light, like a pilgrim who has freed himself from a backpack full of rocks. Nicodemus soon followed suit. Both moved to smaller houses and sold most of their things.

Detaching Ourselves from Relationships: When It Hurts to Love

If seeking permanence in what is essentially impermanent leads to unhappiness, it should come as no surprise that misunderstood personal relationships can also feel like a backpack full of rocks.

They say that someone with fifty friends has fifty headaches. The pressure to accumulate and retain is not limited to the material realm; it can also be seen in relationships.

Just as belongings get old, break, or cease to interest us, relationships also fluctuate over time. That funny friend we had so much in common with has changed—it might feel like a betrayal—and is now tiresome and never has time for us, and when we do see them, all they do is complain. That person we were so physically attracted to now bores us and we start having eyes for others.

This doesn't mean that all relationships change for the worse. On the contrary, if we love from a state of nonattachment, accepting what each person is in each moment, we will be able to share the adventure of life.

Heracleitus, one of the first Greek philosophers, insisted that the only thing permanent is change. Expecting someone to stay the same, in addition to being a fantasy, is also to misunderstand the essential dynamic of life.

Beyond this, a major source of pain in relationships is expectations. From the moment we expect another to react or reciprocate our feelings in a certain way, we are planting the seed of suffering.

You text a friend who doesn't respond as quickly as you'd hoped or in the way you wanted. You get mad and say things like, "If I were them, I would have . . ."

In romantic relationships, waiting for the other person to change to conform to our needs is a constant source of arguments and criticism.

Expectations pave another road to unhappiness.

When our partners change in ways we don't want them to, we suffer.

When our partners don't change in the ways we would like them to, we suffer.

In both cases, you can blame the other for your unhappiness, even though the problem is inside you and is called attachment. Fritz Perls, the cofounder of Gestalt therapy, gave us a prayer for freeing ourselves from this painful trap. It goes like this:

I do my thing and you do your thing.
I am not in this world to live up to your expectations,
And you are not in this world to live up to mine.
You are you, and I am I,
and if by chance we find each other, it's beautiful.
If not, it can't be helped.

Detaching Ourselves from Knowledge

Beyond attachments to things and relationships, there is a third kind of attachment, which causes as much suffering as the previous ones. This kind is born of the need to know more or better than others, to always be right. Having preconceived ideas about the world—in other words, being attached to our own knowledge—is another source of constant friction with others.

In our daily lives, we see a lot of conflict that stems from this third variety of attachment. Two examples:

- Arguments over politics and religion, in which each person fights for their "truth," not realizing that it is only an opinion
- Anger about what goes on around us because it doesn't conform to our preconceived notions of how things ought to be

The more rigid our thoughts, the greater our unhappiness, since our unhappiness will deepen every time reality does not conform to how we think it should be.

Getting rid of our fixed ideas, assuming that it is much better to live in peace than to be right, is the third detachment that will bring us closer to a life of serenity.

TO CROSS, NOT TO CLING TO

"Mendicants, I will teach you a simile of the teaching as a raft: for crossing over, not for holding on. Listen and apply your mind well, I will speak."

"Yes, sir," they replied. The Buddha said this:

"Suppose there was a person traveling along the road. They'd see a large deluge whose near shore was dubious and perilous, while the far shore was a sanctuary free of peril. But there was no ferryboat or bridge for crossing over. They'd think, 'Why don't I gather grass, sticks, branches, and leaves and make a raft? Riding on the raft, and paddling with my hands and feet, I can safely reach the far shore.' And so they'd do exactly that. And when they'd crossed over to the far shore, they'd think, 'This raft has been very helpful to me. Riding on the raft, and paddling with my hands and feet, I have safely crossed over to the far shore. Why don't I hoist it on my head or pick it up on my shoulder and go wherever I want?' What do you think, mendicants? Would that person be doing what should be done with that raft?"

"No, sir."

"And what, mendicants, should that person do with

the raft? When they'd crossed over they should think, 'This raft has been very helpful to me. . . . Why don't I beach it on dry land or set it adrift on the water and go wherever I want?' That's what that person should do with the raft.

In the same way, I have taught a simile of the teaching as a raft: for crossing over, not for holding on. By understanding the simile of the raft, you will even give up the teachings, let alone what is against the teachings."

(*Dhammā* in the plural refers back to "those teachings" [*tesaṁ dhammānaṁ*] of the nine categories. Accordingly, when this simile is invoked at MN 38:14.1, it is in reference to views. The pair *dhamma* and *adhamma* usually means "the teaching" and "against the teaching" [e.g. AN 2.104]. The negative form has a stronger sense than simply "not the teaching"; it implies there is something unnatural, in conflict with the way the world is.)

—Buddha, *Majjhima Nikaya**

Detaching Ourselves from the Ego

Our ego is like a fortress that we must defend. If it is small, there will be fewer places from which it can be attacked. If

---

* From *Middle Discourses* by Bhikkhu Sujato (Australia, SuttaCentral, 2018).

it is wide and unwieldy, we will be forced to stand guard at every door, which will be exhausting.

The need to be someone who stands out and receives the recognition of others is a fourth kind of attachment that causes us pain and suffering. Given that others have their own ego and likewise defend their own fortress, there will be no lack of occasions when we feel undervalued, attacked, or discredited.

The origin of this source of pain and misunderstanding is the illusion that you are a separate entity from the world, without understanding that we all essentially have the same needs: obtaining food and shelter, being loved and respected, and feeling like our presence in the world matters.

There is a famous incident when a pilgrim approached Ramana Maharshi, whom we met in the chapter devoted to self-knowledge, and asked him: "How should we treat others?"

"Others do not exist," answered Maharshi.

With this statement, he meant that in reality, we are all one. We will explore this idea in greater depth in the next chapter.

Advaita

....

Non-Duality

*A*dvaita is usually translated as "non-duality," in the sense that there is no separation between the *atman*, the soul, and *Brahman*, which is divinity. This branch of Hinduism questions the very principle of reality, like in the movie *The Matrix*, by analyzing the three states of consciousness: wakefulness, dreaming, and deep sleep.

Just as we assume that when we dream, we enter an illusory world, how can we know whether what we experience when we are awake is not also a dream?

From the Veil of Maya to Moksha

"Nothing is real," sang the Beatles in "Strawberry Fields Forever," an idea in keeping with this vision of the Advaita. More than two millennia ago, Plato himself suggested in his theory of the cave that the things we see are merely shadows of a fundamental truth.

From this point of view, material things, people, and the whole universe are only illusions, if we consider them as separate from ourselves. The only thing that exists is a *whole* of which we form part. In this vision, the ego stops making sense.

Maya is the Sanskrit term for describing illusion, the mirage created by the human intellect, which resides in the *avidya*, defined as "ignorance" or "false knowledge." Under the yoke of maya and avidya, the intellect is dissociated from the whole, and is identified with its self and its body. Reality thus appears as duality, something separate from God.

When the human being frees themselves from ignorance through the realization of their being, they live in a state of moksha, the liberation brought by being free of desires or aspirations.

This is how a person realizes that they *are not this or that* but that they are pure being, pure consciousness, pure love. They abandon the suffering of duality and achieve limitless freedom. The ego is no longer there to experience and divide.

That is when they wake up.

Non-duality can be reached through reflection, religious or meditative practice, or contact with nature.

These practices allow us to experience the feeling of being part of something much larger than ourselves. When we gaze at the spectacular night sky, when we walk through a thick forest, when we are moved by a work of art, we feel that we are merging into an almost total experience, in which the line between viewer and viewed disappears.

These are moments of non-duality, when we stop seeing ourselves as separate from the whole, and become an integral part of it.

Advaita and Flow

For Advaita, material things, people, and time itself are an illusion. All possibilities coexist simultaneously, and time is simply a human means of not getting lost in the chaos.

When we merge with life, however, that no longer matters. The experience of flow—described masterfully by Mihaly Csikszentmihalyi in his book of the same name—allows us to disconnect from the ego and its mental noise, and from time itself. The doer merges with what they are doing. Thus, an hour seems like an instant because we have transcended the dual mentality.

A few tips for achieving this valuable state of flow, which, in addition to eliding duality, leads us to excellence and happiness:

1. Do only one thing at a time, with all your passion and your five senses. Multitasking is a sworn enemy of flow.

2. Pay full attention. You can practice this with something as simple as reading a book. Each time something distracts you from your reading, return to it with discipline.

3. Eliminate all distractions during the experience: cell phones or any device connected to the internet; thoughts that take us into the past or future. All of these will interfere with flow. If something bothers or disturbs you, note it somewhere and give yourself over to the experience, free of that burden.

4. According to Csikszentmihalyi, what you do should be neither very easy nor very difficult. If it is too easy, you run the risk of doing it on autopilot and losing your focus. If it is too difficult, you can experience a block. Raising the bar a little higher than what you've achieved in the past will keep you motivated. About this, Hemingway once said, "Sometimes I have good luck and write better than I can."

Old Teachers, New Teachers

Advaita Vedanta is thought to have been shaped by the Indian thinker Adi Shankara, born in the eighth century and inspired by the Upanishads, the texts that are the basis of Hinduism.

A student of Gaudapada, who asserted that "there is neither dissolution nor creation, there is none seeking liberation, and none liberated, and nobody is enslaved," Shankara had many followers, but four of his disciples became especially popular: Padmapada, Suresvara, Hastamalaka, and Totaka.

Each of them gave a name to the four great monasteries that were established in India and still exist today.

THE FIRST MOVIE IN SANSKRIT

In 1983, *Adi Shankaracharya*—the first movie fully filmed in Sanskrit—was released, and garnered numerous prizes in India. This singular two-hour biopic tells of the life of the pioneer of Advaita. Born into a wealthy, happy family, the young Shankara developed a great thirst for knowledge following the death of his father. After letting his mother know his decision, he began his spiritual quest by entering a monastery.

In modern times, the principles of the Advaita school were adopted by Ramana Maharshi, whom we mentioned in the previous chapter and in the chapter devoted to self-knowledge.

After an adolescence full of introspection, Maharshi experienced his own death and rebirth at age sixteen. Then, a mysterious word floated into his mind: *Arunachala*. He would later discover that this was the name of a hill in Tamil Nadu.

A year later, in 1896, he moved to this enigmatic place, where at first he would meditate in temples and caverns, seeking purification, silence, and detachment, until he founded his own ashram.

Among his most famous disciples would be Papaji, who

was born in Punjab and who met Maharshi in 1944 and asked him the same question that he had posed to all the gurus he had met during his search.

"Can you show me God? And if not, do you know anyone who can?"

"I cannot show you God nor allow you to see him," Maharshi told him, "because God is not an object that can be seen. God is the subject. He is the seer. Do not worry about objects that can be seen. Discover who is the seer."

In a second encounter, upon looking Maharshi in the eye, Papaji finally achieved enlightenment, abandoning duality forever.

Two of Maharshi's most important ideas:

• Words can point toward truth, but they are not the truth. To access holiness, the true door is silence.

• Enlightenment, the experience of non-duality, will arrive effortlessly if you neither stimulate nor reject any thought.

Papaji's most popular student was Mooji. He was originally from Jamaica, but his ashram is located in the province of Alentejo in Portugal. Mooji shares Maharshi's self-exploration—asking yourself over and over, *Who am I?*—and

Papaji's conviction that duality ends when you stop struggling to maintain an identity.

For Mooji, enlightenment is not something reached after a difficult process, but something we carry inside us. All we need to do is let go of the preconceived ideas that distort our vision of the world, especially the idea that there is a separation between subject and object.

The London Advaita School

In line with these teachers, the British journalist Tony Parsons explains in his book *As It Is* that his spiritual awakening came about spontaneously as he walked through a London park.

After a lifetime of anxiety, worrying constantly about what might happen, he realized that he was already what he was seeking. He always had been—he just hadn't realized until that moment. To achieve this insight, all he needed to do was leave mind games aside and direct all his attention to walking.

For the first time, Parsons felt that every step was different and unique and would never be repeated in the same way. As he became absorbed by an exercise as simple and human as walking, everything became clear, and he gained a sense of total peace and presence.

Time, his mental projections, and even the walker himself disappeared. Parsons was now one with each of his steps, but also with everything that existed in the world. He had achieved unity.

He began to talk about his experiences in places as ordinary as a London pub, where he soon set up an informal Advaita circle. One of his disciples, Richard Sylvester, had experienced a similar awakening in a train station.

At the end of one of his meetings with Sylvester, Parsons embraced him and said, "I hope you die soon," an unusual statement and one that Sylvester would adopt as the title of his own book. What was Parsons trying to say?

Essentially, he was saying that to awaken to a new life, you must kill the old one. The death of the ego gives birth to non-duality, the state in which we cease to feel the pain of separation.

And What Use Is Advaita to Me?

Perhaps the experiences of Maharshi and Papaji, or that of these urban Advaita explorers, aren't for everyone, but they are useful for anyone who aspires to live a life as free and happy as possible, which is the goal of this book.

To this end, we are going to bring the teachings of this millenarian school to the realm of everyday life:

- The fuller you are of ego, the more suffering, attachment, fear, and worry you will experience. Any activity that allows you to forget yourself, even if it is a simple walk in the park, will result in serenity and more freedom in your life.

- Filling yourself with others is another way of emptying yourself of yourself. Altruism contributes to dissolving the ego, and at the same time helps us achieve peace and fulfillment. When you are feeling down, do you ever have the experience of your spirits being revived by the need to help someone who was suffering? Being like an empty shell that is filled by others is another highway to wholeness.

- When we enter a state of flow, we merge with the activity and break down the barrier between the doer and what is being done. To achieve this, all you have to do is give yourself fully to your passion, with all five senses and without distractions, but also without any agenda or expectations.

• Being conscious of the Universe is another way of overcoming duality. Whether by reading books or experiencing other ways of getting outside yourself, realizing the extent of your own insignificance, in the warmth of a minor sun in a peripheral galaxy among the billions that exist, is an antidote to the ego and the problems it generates.

This awakening or enlightenment does not make us smaller. On the contrary, it allows us to merge with the grandeur of all that exists, multiplying our possibilities in an immense playing field.

We like to connect it to the beginning of this poem written by Fernando Pessoa in 1928, under the pseudonym Álvaro de Campos:

I am nothing.
I'll never be anything.
I couldn't want to be something.
Apart from that, I have in me all the dreams in the
world.

The Universal Laws of Happiness

Traveling the world, we have learned that variety is the spice of life. But even more than we enjoy discovering what makes each culture unique, we like to find the connecting threads that unite all the world's cultures.

Why, for example, are nearly all friendly greetings in different parts of the planet accompanied by some kind of hand gesture?

In India, when we say *namaste*, we place our hands together in front of us. In Korean and Japanese culture, the bow is performed with the hands in front or to the side in a position visible to the other person. In China and in other cultures, we shake hands.

Whether there is physical contact or not, even with variation in the forms and meaning of each greeting, the common pattern we can observe is that both people are showing each other their hands. Why?

As much as it may surprise us, this is to show that we are not holding a weapon. Though carrying a weapon is rare in contemporary society, showing our empty hands has remained in the human subconscious. For this reason, greeting someone verbally with one's hands in one's pockets is considered rude practically everywhere.

This is just one example of a human behavior that evolved in unison, all over the planet.

As with greetings, there are laws, norms, and traditions that have been passed down for millennia through oral or written stories, or in religious or philosophical texts, in places thousands of miles apart. Yet despite this, we find universal parallels.

Since humans are similar everywhere, we tend to have the same problems no matter where we live. So it makes sense that humans everywhere have come up with similar ways of coexisting in peace and happiness.

The Six Enemies and the Seven Deadly Sins

Just as the Catholic Church defines the seven deadly sins, Hindu theology defines the six enemies of the mind, called *arishadvarga*.

THE UNIVERSAL LAWS OF HAPPINESS

Saint Thomas Aquinas described the deadly sins as "those to which human nature is most inclined."

Hinduism's six enemies of the mind are those temptations that prevent people from achieving their fourth purushartha—moksha, or liberation from ignorance.

The Six Enemies	The Seven Deadly Sins
wrath (*krodha*)	wrath
arrogance or pride (*mada*)	pride
desire or lust (*kama*)	lust
jealousy or envy (*matsarya*)	envy
greed (*lobha*)	greed
delusion (*moha*)	-
-	gluttony
-	sloth

The first five map onto each other almost perfectly. It is curious to see how two different traditions, which evolved over thousands of years in different parts of the world, are in agreement on the vices that tend to lead human beings down a damaging path.

We cannot live a happy life if we allow ourselves to be carried away by anger. Likewise, an excess of pride will make us arrogant. If we do not master our desires and instead allow them to dominate us, we may fall prey to lust. Similarly, we understand that it is healthier to focus on our own lives than to envy others or what they have. Realizing when we have enough and not letting ourselves be led by greed is the path to peace and generosity.

We are probably in agreement about all of this.

Delusion (moha), which is sometimes explained as illusion or delirium, does not have a corresponding deadly sin. In fact, it is a concept very particular to the Hindu worldview. It refers to the fact that we are deceived, since we almost always view reality through a misty window.

When we look at the world, it is tinted by our own perspective.

It is difficult for us to see reality the way it is because our experiences tend to be colored by our ego and our emotions. It is important to be aware of this in order to make decisions that help us see our situation with more clarity.

We do not see the world as it is, but as we are. But the good news is that we can shape what we are, and also our vision of life, from moment to moment.

To finish with the list, gluttony and sloth feature among the seven deadly sins, but they do not have an exact correspondence to any of the six enemies.

Although they are not considered by Hinduism, they do appear on the list of the five obstacles in the Pali Canon in Theravada Buddhism.

The Five Obstacles

The five obstacles in the Theravada tradition, which is the oldest school of Buddhism, have the power to throw us off course on the path to virtue. This can happen both when we meditate and when we try to live a virtuous and purpose-driven life.

The five obstacles are:

1. **Laziness or lethargy** (*thina-middha*): allowing ourselves to be guided by the law of minimal effort instead of doing what we can and should do. This corresponds to sloth in the seven deadly sins.

2. **Sensory desires** (*kama*): being guided by pleasure through any of the five senses (sight, touch, sound, smell, taste). The pleasures of the palate correspond to gluttony in the seven deadly sins.

3. **Hatred, resentment, hostility** (*byapada*): holding feelings of hatred toward the world or other people.

4. **Worry or preoccupation** (*uddhacca-kukkucca*): feeding the worries that prevent us from finding serenity in our hearts and minds.

5. **Doubt** (*vicikiccha*): lacking faith in ourselves to make decisions, which can lead to paralysis.

These five obstacles divert us from our life's purpose.

To counteract the five obstacles, the Theravada tradition describes five antidotes that can help us when we find ourselves trapped in a situation with few ways out.

The five antidotes are:

1. **Thinking intentionally about action to avoid laziness:** Examining the reasons why we are falling prey to lethargy will help us make decisions to be proactive and to overcome inertia and the kind of autopilot that leads to idleness.

2. **Concentrating on a single important thing (*ekaggata*) to avoid physical and sensory desires:** When we feel that we are allowing ourselves to be driven too much by pleasure, bringing our atten-

tion to something unrelated to that pleasure lets us overcome the temptation of the senses for which human beings have such a weakness.

3. **Focusing on well-being (*piti*) to avoid malice or hatred:** When we sense that we are being conquered by feelings of anger, resentment, or regret, we can reorient our attention toward the good things we have in our lives. In the case of hatred or envy of other people, we can use the same method to make a list of their virtues. This will change our way of seeing them.

4. **Non-sensory pleasures (*sukha*) to avoid worries:** Seeking non-sensory pleasures (cultivating the spirit, learning about the world by reading or being guided by teachers and mentors, developing our artistic abilities, caring for our loved ones) will help us to feel well and without worries, no matter what situation we find ourselves in.

5. **Detailed analysis of the situation (*vicara*) to avoid doubt:** A simple and practical technique to overcome uncertainty is to write down the advantages and disadvantages of two options we have before us. The simple act of making a list will help us make decisions.

Obstacle	Antidote
Laziness	Orient ourselves toward action and be proactive to avoid laziness.
Sensory desires	Concentrate on a single important thing to avoid attachments.
Hatred and hostility	Focus on well-being—our own and that of others—to avoid malice and hatred.
Preoccupation and worry	Cultivate non-sensory pleasures to avoid worries.
Doubt	Analyze the situation in detail to avoid uncertainty.

Balancing the Four Purusharthas

The reader with a critical mind might have noticed what seem like contradictions:

- Kama (pleasures of life) is one of the purusharthas (human goals) in the first chapter of this book, but it is also considered one of the five obstacles.
- Those who focus on moksha (self-realization or enlightenment) with all their intent will have to make sacrifices in all the other areas of their life.

You are not the first to notice this tension. The four purusharthas have been the subject of debate among scholars and
philosophers for a long time. The general consensus is that
when in doubt, we should prioritize dharma (righteousness).

The philosopher Daya Krishna, in his book *Indian Philosophy: A Counter Perspective*, has a more nuanced take on
purushartha:

> Is it to be taken, for example, in a descriptive sense, that
> is, as describing what men actually pursue in their life?
> Or is it a prescriptive word which suggests what men ought
> to pursue in order to be worthy of being human? *Artha*
> and *kāma* as examples of *puruṣārthas* tend to suggest
> the former, while *dharma* and *mokṣa* lead to the latter
> interpretation. There does not seem much sense in say-
> ing one ought to pursue *artha* or *kāma*, as one naturally
> pursues them and needs no great exhortation to do so.

In other words, we have a natural tendency to pursue
artha and kama, while for dharma and moksha we need to
develop discipline and be intentional about it.

Keeping in mind the four purusharthas, ask yourself:

• Is my life out of balance?

If the answer is yes, write down the answers to these follow-up questions:

- Am I living a life in which I tend to focus only on pleasures and love (kama)?
- Am I living a life in which I focus only on wealth and money (artha)?
- Am I living a life in which I focus only on my duties (dharma)?
- Am I living a life in which I focus only on my own self-realization (moksha)?

The answers to these questions will help you to notice your tendencies and make adjustments. Well-being and happiness for yourself and your loved ones can be found in balance.

"Virtue is the golden mean between two vices, the one of excess and the other of deficiency." —Aristotle

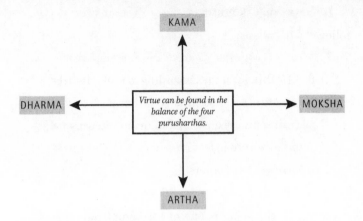

The Four Agreements

Although they belong to the sphere of psychology and personal development and not to any religion, there are a few insights we want to share with you because they have freed us from mental suffering on more than one occasion. The second principle we will look at is especially helpful, but we think the other three also are highly valuable.

In his book *The Four Agreements*, Don Miguel Ruiz presents four principles for living a happy life based on Toltec culture. According to the author, with whom we had a long and friendly telephone conversation, in order to escape suffering, we should commit to these agreements.

Let's see what they are:

1. *Be careful with your words.* Try to be impeccable in everything you say. According to Ruiz, "impeccable words" are those that do no harm. To live in peace, it is necessary to maintain our integrity by acting in accordance with what we say, as much to ourselves as to others.

    Parallels to other traditions:

    • Not lying is one of the commandments of Christianity and Judaism.

    • In other traditions, lying is not a sin per se, but each time we say something untrue or that can be harmful to others, it will have consequences for our karma.

    • Gandhi is said to have put it this way: "Happiness is when what you think, what you do, and what you say are in harmony."

2. *Don't take it personally.* When you feel attacked by someone or something, do not take it as something personal. Every individual sees the world through their situation in life, and what they do or say speaks only of that person, not of us. Ruiz points out that this second agreement helps to

dispel our feelings of anger, hatred, jealousy, and envy.

Parallels to other traditions:

- As we saw in the first section of this chapter, anger, jealousy, and envy are among the deadly sins and also the six enemies of Hinduism. This agreement will help us keep those undesirable feelings at bay.

3. *Do not assume.* It is a mistake to imagine what other people are thinking about you or others, since, among other reasons, you simply do not know. Trying to guess what others think serves only to increase our suffering. We almost always see the world through a distorted lens that we believe to be the truth.

Parallels to other traditions:

- This agreement corresponds to delusion (moha), one of the six enemies of Hinduism. Making assumptions about too many things, both in the world around us and with other people, is a poison for the mind because it brings suffering.

4. *Do it as well as possible.* This agreement is an invitation to make the maximum effort at every moment

of your life. The Japanese have a term for this, *Ganbatte*, which can be translated as "Do your best." You can apply this principle when it comes to how you treat both yourself and others.

Parallels to other traditions:

- Doing things as well as possible and treating others in the best way possible is implicit in practically all religions. Let's remember the following Christian commandment: "Thou shalt love thy neighbor as thyself."

- To do our best in life, we must not fall prey to any of the six enemies of Hinduism, or to the temptations of the seven deadly sins, or allow ourselves to be paralyzed by the five obstacles.

Improve Your First Purushartha (Dharma) with the Franklin Method

Dharma, the first purushartha, is about acting according to law, with rightness, moral duty, and virtue.

It is not easy to be a virtuous person. All of us struggle

to balance our emotions and self-interest while at the same time taking into account what we ought to do.

Benjamin Franklin devised a system devoted to thirteen virtues that he felt he should develop. The Founding Father and polymath used a notebook organized around the seven days of the week, each week dedicated to the cultivation of a specific virtue. Each day he had to demonstrate with his actions that he had exercised one of these virtues—for example, patience—and then check off a box indicating that he had completed that day's task.

Only if he racked up seven check marks in one week did he allow himself to tackle a new virtue the following week. When he managed to cultivate the thirteen virtues, he started over.

"Happiness," Franklin is thought to have said, "consists more in the small conveniences of pleasures that occur every day, than in great pieces of good fortune that happen but seldom to a man in the course of his life."

As a final exercise, we suggest you try a simplified version of the Franklin method, focusing on one thing you don't like about yourself.

- Choose a habit or attitude you would like to give up because it contributes nothing positive to your life, much less to happiness.

- Make a list of small things that you can change and actions you can take to free yourself from this burden.
- Set yourself a goal of undertaking one of those actions to free yourself from the thing that you do not like.
- If you manage to do this for seven days, treat yourself to a reward.

Karma

....

The History of Your Lives

There are many different points of view on the meaning of karma. For some Indian religions, this law of cause and effect transcends one's life and influences the next reincarnation. To put it simply, if we have made spiritual progress in this life, then in the next one, we will be reborn as a superior being until we are freed from the cycle of birth and death. Whereas if we have not lived a virtuous life, we will be reborn in the form of an inferior being, perhaps even as an animal.

As we will see in this chapter, however, even if we do not believe in transcendence, the law of karma can be an ally in changing the way we understand the world and progress through life.

Karma Police

The British band Radiohead warned in their song "Karma Police" that we would reap what we sowed in their own particular description of retribution.

When we assume that every action has a consequence, our fortune becomes the fruit of each and every one of the thousands of decisions we make, day after day. People who find themselves adrift are characterized by a lack of awareness of this law of cause and effect that governs their lives.

If something goes badly, they attribute it to bad luck, the unkindness of others, or the injustice that reigns in the world at large. This lack of responsibility for our fate makes us into slaves of circumstance and sometimes of superstition.

We all know people who knock on wood or perform some other ritual to summon good luck, forgetting that we create our own luck from moment to moment with each of our actions, words, and beliefs.

If you want karma on your side, you must submit to its law, and when something goes badly or causes you pain, ask yourself these questions:

- How have I contributed to this situation?
- How else could I have acted to achieve a different result?
- What should I change in the future for the wheel of life to turn in my favor?

When we clearly see the consequences of our actions, karma is the light that allows us to discover our own nature and the whole spectrum of progress. In this sense, it is the awakening of conscience we need, and an invitation to break out of our vicious cycles and improve ourselves.

Questions for Adjusting Our Karma

"My actions are my only true belongings. I cannot escape the consequences of my actions. They are the ground on which I stand," the Vietnamese monk Thich Nhat Hanh reminds us, quoting the fifth of the Buddha's Five Remembrances.*

Though many Westerners connect the law of karma to

---

* From *Understanding Our Mind* by Thich Nhat Hanh (New York: Parallax Press, 2002): 46.

Buddhist philosophy, in fact it predates Buddhism. It is mentioned in the *Chandogya Upanishad*, dating back to between the eighth and sixth centuries BC. This second of the Hindu sacred books has permeated Buddhism, Jainism, and other religions.

In Sanskrit, the language of the Upanishads and all of Vedic literature, *karma* means "action," and that is how all these dharmic religions interpret it: like a cosmic energy of effect, in which every act yields a consequence.

Regardless of our religious orientation, the responsibility of each person to build their karma is essential. Karma lies not only in actions but also in words and thoughts, since both are the seeds of future actions and thus generate karma.

As Renaissance genius Leonardo da Vinci reminded us, "Everything connects to everything else."

Infinite knot

It is no coincidence that an infinite knot is used to represent the karmic cycle, whose dynamic, as described by the writer and doctor Deepak Chopra, flows as an experience that creates memory, which in turn generates imagination and desire, which then triggers new actions.

To take control of our karma, we must therefore question the suitability of:

- *Our actions*, which generate consequences that will force us to react in a certain way. Am I acting in the best way for myself and others?
- *Our words*, since these can cause happiness or unhappiness, closeness or distance, success or failure. As with our actions, our fate depends on our words. As Don Miguel Ruiz asked in *The Four Agreements*: Am I being impeccable with my words?
- *Our thoughts and desires*, since they set the direction of our words and deeds, thus making up our reality. Am I thinking clearly? Do my desires correspond to what I really need in order to be fulfilled and to make others happy?

Answering these questions periodically is the best way to adjust our karma.

INSTANT KARMA

Hinduism speaks of three kinds of karma, depending on the moment of action. *Prarabdha* is karma manifested while we act; *sanchita* stays in our mind and arises in future situations that take us back to that original gesture; and *agami* appears in the future after a repeated action. However it happened, consequences will come.

This boomerang factor can have comic and contradictory aspects. For example, there are humorous videos in which people who have acted unpleasantly immediately reap what they sow. There is a German saying that describes this kind of instant karma: "God punishes small sins right away"—for example, when we shout or behave angrily toward someone and then immediately hit our head or bump into something.

Wanting someone to receive their karma affects the karma, whether positively or negatively, of the person expressing this.

In his song "Instant Karma!" John Lennon sang that "we all shine on," alluding to enlightenment, when we are fully conscious of cause and effect and can therefore live our lives doing good.

Stop Repeating History

To have good karma, our experience, imagination, and desire should be voluntarily oriented toward goodness, because everything we offer the world influences us. To achieve this, we must cultivate positive habits. As the *Brihadaranyaka Upanishad* says, "A man of good works will become good."

On the other side of the scale would be those who always trip over the same stone, just as we read in the *Dhammapada*, which preserves the words of the Buddha: "Fools of little wit are enemies unto themselves as they move about doing evil deeds, the fruits of which are bitter."

Since we can influence our karma only through acceptance and taking responsibility for our behavior, one of its laws reminds us: what you refuse to accept will keep happening to you.

Therefore, karma—what happens to us in our lives—is a kind of school for teaching us how to have a clear conscience.

There is a well-known Tibetan fable that the lama Nyoshul Khenpo used to tell in five parts.

I. I walk down the street. There is a deep hole in the sidewalk. I fall in. I am lost . . . I am helpless. It isn't my fault. It takes me forever to find a way out.

II. I walk down the same street. There is a deep hole in the sidewalk. I pretend I don't see it. I fall in again. I can't believe I am in the same place. But it isn't my fault. It still takes a long time to get out.

III. I walk down the same street. There is a deep hole in the sidewalk. I see it is there. I still fall in . . . It's a habit. My eyes are open. I know where I am. It is my fault. I get out immediately.

IV. I walk down the same street. There is a deep hole in the sidewalk. I walk around it.

V. I walk down a different street.

Some Karmic Commandments

As we have seen, the law of karma is not a punishment but rather an opportunity to learn, and to live consciously and be free to choose one's path, like the person in the fable about the hole in the sidewalk. Our present actions determine our future and even make up for past mistakes, like in the movie *Back to the Future*.

Unlike in the movie, however, we cannot go back to the past and change it, but what we can do is learn from it so we can act differently in the future.

To do so, we can follow these karmic commandments:

1. *You reap what you sow. Or, you get what you give.* This is the basis of the law of cause and effect. In some spiritual traditions it is said that evil returns ten times over.

2. *Practice kindness and generosity.* Our mission is to create the best for ourselves and our surroundings, which are inseparable from us.

3. *What you refuse to accept will keep happening to you.* Like in the story about the hole, we must be humble enough to recognize our mistakes and be able to grow as human beings.

4. *Take responsibility.* When numerous unpleasant things happen in our lives, we should look at what we carry within us, since our outer life is often a mirror of how we are inside.

5. *Understand the connection.* Realize that everything is connected and that, as with the butterfly effect, any minor gesture can unleash a greater positive or negative result.

6. *Focus.* Do not try to approach everything all at once. For our life lessons to be authentic, we should narrow down our efforts with small goals that will help us improve.

7. *Be present.* The here and now is where you cultivate your karma. Stop being anchored to the past.

8. *Correct your behavior to achieve change.* Just as the saying mistakenly attributed to Einstein goes, "The definition of insanity is doing the same thing over and over again and expecting different results."

9. *Be patient.* Good karma grows slowly and silently, and takes time to bear its fruit.

10. *Keep up the effort.* Being virtuous for just one day is like a drop in the ocean. We can shape our lives only through consciousness and consistency.

Rebooting the Operating System of Our Lives

When we give the best of ourselves unconditionally, karma follows in our wake. The Taoist philosopher Lao-tzu explains how we can reboot the operating system of our lives: "Following the Universal Way means practicing selflessness and extending virtue to the world unconditionally. In this way

KARMA: THE HISTORY OF YOUR LIVES

one not only eliminates the heavy contamination accumulated throughout many lifetimes but may also bring about the possibility of restoring one's original divine nature . . ."

Karma is like a story we express in a versatile format: life. A responsible life based on personal improvement, with no thought for punishment or reward, is the blank page that karma wants to remind us of at every moment.

And on this blank page, we can choose whether to express negativity and resentment or light and love.

It is said that Ananda, Buddha's disciple, once greeted his teacher and said, "This is half of the holy life, lord: admirable friendship, admirable companionship, admirable camaraderie."

"Don't say that, Ananda. Don't say that," answered his teacher. "Admirable friendship, admirable companionship, admirable camaraderie is actually the whole of the holy life."

Every action, every word, and every thought feeds karma. Each of them is a seed that will grow into the flower of unhappiness or of joy.

Samsara and Nirvana

I f we explore the nature of the Universe, the first charac-
teristic we take for granted is its dualities: light and dark,
life and death, positive and negative are inseparable.

We can try to understand that the meaning of everything is found in difference by thinking for a moment
about the soothing creation of a mandala, which represents
precisely this universal infinity and harmony by balancing
various visual elements. For example, we can visualize one
of the best-known mandalas, the *taijitu*, with its comple-
mentary yin and yang, which is the symbol of this duality
for Taoism.

In the same way, we can also understand that suffering
and freedom form part of this dual equation. Or what
amounts to the same: samsara and nirvana make up the cycle
of life. The Sanskrit root of *samsara* means "passing through
different states" or even "wandering," since it alludes to a

path that moves from attachment and confusion until reaching the deep inner peace of *nirvana*.

The Long and Winding Road of the Soul

As Paul McCartney lamented in the Beatles song "The Long and Winding Road," when we talk about life and the ups and downs and learning experiences that come one after another, we sometimes reach a state of exhaustion and a feeling that life is more than we can handle.

For some spiritual traditions, the accumulated karmic debt that stems from our most uncertain actions, words, and thoughts makes us travel in a circle of births and deaths in various bodies until we have paid it.

The flow of reincarnation teaches us life lessons so that we can become optimal versions of ourselves. "Long is the night to him who is awake; long is the mile to him who is tired; long is life to the foolish who do not know the true law," said the Buddha, this "law" being the aspiration to improve and fulfill our potential, awakening our conscience.

But it is not necessary to believe in life after death to make the journey from samsara to nirvana, from unconsciousness to consciousness, from darkness to light. We can travel this path within a single existence, even within the day we are currently living through.

To remove the stones in front of us and clear our path, we can ask ourselves these questions:

- What are the stones obstructing my path? (These can be beliefs, bad habits, mistaken actions.)
- If I am conscious of these, why have I not removed them?
- How am I going to act from now on to clear my path toward nirvana?

WANDERING LOVERS

In a scene in Francis Ford Coppola's brilliant film adaptation of Bram Stoker's novel *Dracula*, the vampire par excellence confesses to his beloved Mina, "I have crossed oceans of time to find you." This is a love born lifetimes ago, considering the count's immortality. Despite this, the lovers still recognize each other.

From a spiritual point of view, immortal longing is the fusion with the divine that brings relief from pain and the ability to live in eternal love with the Universe.

Until this communion, or nirvana, lovers who roam in samsara can also find each other again as "twin flames" who share karma; loves at first sight who light us up and make us experience déjà vu, as if we had already lived that moment. It is in moments like this when we say things like, "I feel as if we have known each other for a long time."

What if this means that our love came from another life?

Some people are taken by surprise, while others, aware that samsara will bring them together, lay foundations for the meeting, like Shah Jahan, who upon the death of his favorite wife in 1631 built in her honor the Taj Mahal, where he was buried beside his beloved so that they could walk the same path together forever after.

We experience a constant succession of feelings, impressions, and moments that stimulate the flow of karma. Hindus believe that for as long as the soul lives under the illusion (maya) that the body and the temporary world are everything, it will suffer in samsara for being ignorant of the fact that we cannot be separate from the divine.

Walking in Circles: The Wheel of Samsara

The *samsaracakra*, or wheel of life, illustrates the passage through six states, referred to as realms, until nirvana is reached. In each one, we learn to discard the bad and embrace the virtuous to progress toward liberation from suffering.

It is said that Buddha recorded the details of all his past lives in the moment of his enlightenment. In other words, his experience in each of the six realms of existence appeared clearly in his memory:

1. The realm of the *devas*, or gods, full of pride and happiness
2. The realm of the *asuras*, or demigods, known for jealousy and envy
3. The realm of the *manusas*, or humans, where attachment, desire, doubt, and passion are typical
4. The realm of the *tiryaks*, or animals, characterized by prejudice and stupidity
5. The realm of the *pretas*, or hungry ghosts, greedy and possessive
6. The realm of the *narakas*, or denizens of hell, full of suffering and anger

Along this long and winding path, we develop spiritually through meditation, compassion, and altruism, discovering the happiness that comes from nonattachment. This allows us to take the stairway to nirvana, expressed in the wheel of samsara as the way out into the light, and described by the Tibetan yogi Milarepa, who lived between the eleventh and twelfth centuries, like this:

> *Behold and search your unborn mind;*
> *Seek not for satisfaction in samsara.*
> *I attain all my knowledge through observing the mind*
>   *within—*
> *Those who realize the nature of their own mind know*
> *That the mind itself is Wisdom-Awareness,*
> *And no longer make the mistake of searching for Buddha*
>   *from other sources.*
> *In fact, Buddha cannot be found by searching,*
> *So contemplate your own mind.*
> *This is the highest teaching one can practice.**

---

* From *Benedict's Dharma*, edited by Patrick Henry (New York: Riverhead Books, 2001): 106.

Extinguish Yourself to Shine

Seeing the light at the end of our spiritual tunnel is identified as nirvana, but the word, originally from Pali, can be literally translated as "extinguishing" or "blowing out."

Certainly, we extinguish desire, hatred, and ignorance when our consciousness is set alight inside us, to feel divinity and to detach from our ego and our ties to the material world.

For the philosopher Alan Watts, gaining access to nirvana is a consequence of the relief of the person on the path:

In Sanskrit, nirvana means to blow out, to exhale the breath. Its opposite, desire, is to breathe in. Now, if you breathe in and hold it, you lose your breath; but if you breathe out it comes back to you. So the point is: if you want life, do not cling to it, let it go.*

---

* From Alan Watts, *The Way of Liberation* (New York: Weatherhill, 1983).

ENLIGHTENMENT THROUGH ROCK MUSIC

In the secular world, many people seek a route to calm through creativity and the arts. We cannot finish this chapter without mentioning the band Nirvana, who gave the word its most often repeated modern use, and who seemed to have considered spiritual freedom when choosing their name.

Nirvana's tortured front man, Kurt Cobain, described music as a path to relief from samsara: "Punk is musical freedom. It's saying, doing, and playing what you want. In Webster's terms, 'nirvana' means freedom from pain, suffering, and the external world, and that's pretty close to my definition of Punk Rock."

India is the cradle of spiritual practices that have spread all across the world. From the Hindu tradition, we have taken yoga and meditation as ways to find moksha or *samadhi*, that treasured enlightenment.

In meditation, which we will examine in the third part of this book, the practitioner turns to contemplation, to the repetition of mantras or the creation of mandalas, giving the breath a principal role. The goal is to awaken the bodily, emotional, and mental consciousness to purity.

Having control of your emotions, reconciling yourself to

who you are, and accepting conflict are starting points on the path toward personal nirvana. Meditating regularly, cultivating resilience, empathy, and compassion, encouraging non-attachment, living in the present moment, and acquiring healthy habits will help you clear your most precious "possession," your mind.

In conclusion, the path from samsara to nirvana is a process of personal discovery that leads us toward beauty. As the poet Kahlil Gibran summarizes with exquisite simplicity: "Yes, there is a Nirvanah; it is in leading your sheep to a green pasture, and in putting your child to sleep, and in writing the last line of your poem."*

---

* From *Sand and Foam* by Kahlil Gibran (New York: Knopf, 1926): 217.

III

THE PRACTICE OF HAPPINESS

....

Practical Wisdom from India
for Essential Well-Being

Pranayama

....

Breathing Is Living

In the 1980s, the Framingham Heart Study revealed a striking discovery about the determining factors of longevity. This research into heart disease compiled two decades of data from fifty-two hundred people and concluded that the greatest indicator of life expectancy is not genetics, diet, or exercise, but lung capacity.

After seventy years of research, there was a clear conclusion: larger lungs equal longer lives. With greater lung capacity comes greater longevity, and better health.

The Expansion of Vital Energy

By the time this study was being discussed in the Western world, the benefits of conscious breathing had been known in India for at least five thousand years.

In the area of yoga dedicated to breathing, this was called *pranayama*. In Sanskrit, *prana* means "vital energy," and *ayama* is "expansion." Breathing expands the life force of everyone and increases longevity, just as the Framingham Study demonstrated.

Another accepted theory on the etymology of *pranayama* considers it to be a combination of *prana* and *yama*. This second word means "control," so these breathing exercises represent a technique for controlling each person's vital force.

As Sri Swami Sivananda affirms in his book *The Science of Pranayama*, "Whatever moves or works or has life, is but an expression . . . of prana."

The Science of Breathing

The parasympathetic nervous system is responsible for regulating the functioning of all our organs, in an unconscious way. When we are free of stress and anxiety, the state we are in is known as homeostasis.

Losing this homeostasis can make us enter a state of lethargy, apathy, or even depression. We can also suffer from anxiety and stress while performing any trivial task.

Getting out of this hole is not easy when our parasympathetic nervous system is out of balance. How can we regain control of a system that in theory is uncontrollable?

The only way is through breathing. Usually, we do not need to be conscious of our breathing, but we can choose to take control of it.

Control of our breathing → influence on the parasympathetic nervous system → regulation of stress or hypervigilance (for example, by raising or lowering our heart rate).

There are endless techniques or exercises to control our breathing. Which breathing exercise is right for you?

There are four factors we can adjust when it comes to our breathing:

1. Breathing through the nose or the mouth. In general, we should breathe through the nose, or at least inhale through the nose and exhale through the mouth.
2. The amount of air we inhale and exhale
3. The way we inhale and exhale: whether we concentrate on filling the belly or the chest
4. The rhythm with which we inhale, hold the breath, and exhale

This fourth component is key for controlling our breathing. We can visualize it as follows:

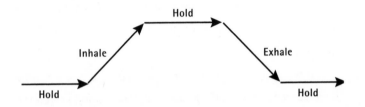

Phases of high or clavicular breathing

Find out which breathing exercise to use according to your mood:

A. If you wake up feeling lethargic and lacking energy and want to get going:

> • The *inhalation* should last longer than the *exhalation*.

B. If you feel very anxious and want to relax:

> • The *exhalation* should last longer than the *inhalation*.

C. If you cannot concentrate and feel somewhat restless:

• The *exhalation* and *inhalation* should last about the same length of time.

HA, THE BREATH OF LIFE

Breathing is understood to be central not only in India but also in other parts of the world. For example, in ancestral Hawaiian culture, there is a greeting in which the so-called *ha*, the air that is breathed, is exchanged. This is done by touching noses with the person you are greeting and inhaling at the same time. Sharing the breath of life is the most profound way of expressing friendship. In Hawaiian culture, the breath is considered one of the keys to good health, since it is believed that the air possesses mana, or spiritual power.

Surya Bhedana

There are eight classic pranayama exercises, but perhaps the most common is the *surya bhedana*, or breathing through the right nostril.

Surya means "sun," and *bhedana* means "perforate" or "enter." In the yogic tradition, the right nostril, or *pingala nadi*, is the portal through which solar energy enters. Its opposite, the left nostril, or *ida nadi*, is the portal of lunar energy. Solar energy is understood as hot or masculine vitality in the body, while lunar energy is calm or feminine vitality.

The practice of surya bhedana is considered energizing, ideal for carrying out in the morning. It stimulates the internal organs around the navel and the root chakra, thus awakening vigorous *kundalini* energy.

The prana enters (bhedana) through the right nostril as solar energy (surya) in the body.

Surya Bhedana Step-by-Step

1. Sit on your yoga mat with your legs crossed, either in *sukhasana* (without crossing your feet) or in *padmasana* (the lotus position). Make sure your spine and head are in a straight line to facilitate the flow of energy through the body.

Vishnu mudra

2. Place your right hand in *vishnu mudra*, with the thumb, ring finger, and pinky extended, and the middle and index fingers bent. Bring the hand to your left nostril and close the nostril with your ring finger.

Gyan mudra

3. Place your left hand in *gyan mudra*, with the tip of the index finger touching the tip of the thumb, forming a circle, and the other three fingers extended.

4. With your left nostril still closed, breathe in through your right nostril.

5. Then close your right nostril with your thumb and hold your breath.

6. Open your left nostril and breathe out.

7. Do ten rounds of breathing—*inhale-hold-exhale*— according to your level:

   • Beginner's level: 1:1:1. Inhale for one second, hold your breath for one second, and exhale for one second.

- Advanced level: 1:4:2. You can move on to the advanced level after two weeks at the beginner's level.

BREATHING AS A TOOL

A simple rule of breathing is that if you spend more time inhaling than exhaling, you are activated. You get warmer, and your heart beats faster. This kind of breathing is sometimes called Breath of Fire and is often practiced in the morning. It is like having coffee. It sends more oxygen into your blood.

On the other hand, exhaling for longer than you inhale relaxes you. This is the kind of breathing practiced at the end of a yoga session when you lie down on the mat.

Another method is called box breathing, and it was devised by the military for combat situations. In this method, the amount of time you inhale equals the amount of time you exhale. This is also a relaxation tool for those with anxiety. It is ideal for preventing an anxiety attack—for example, on a plane. It is easy to do:

1. Inhale for four seconds.
2. Hold your breath for four seconds.
3. Exhale for four seconds.

The 4(inhale):4(hold):4(exhale):4(hold) is ideal for people who are nervous or have anxiety. When you feel nervous, you hyperventilate, which is the opposite of what you should do to keep your calm. This method of breathing prevents hyperventilation because you spend more time holding and exhaling than inhaling.

Sitali Pranayama

If surya bhedana is an energizing breath that activates and warms up the body, *sitali pranayama* is its opposite. *Sitali* is also spelled *sheetali*; *sheet* in Sanskrit means "cold."

Also known as the cooling breath, sitali is ideal for relaxing the body after an intense day. Regular practice cleanses the body, eliminating toxins, stress, excess heat, and emotions that wear us down, such as anger.

Sitali Pranayama Step-by-Step

1. Sit on your yoga mat with your legs crossed or in the lotus position. Make sure your head and spine form a straight line. You can make a gyan mudra with your hands.
2. Breathe deeply three times with an open mouth and exhale through your nose to prepare yourself for sitali breathing.
3. Stick out your tongue and roll it up in the shape of a U.
4. Inhale through your rolled-up tongue, and toward the end of the inhalation, lower your chin to your chest as far as you can. This blocking of the throat is known as *jalandhara bandha.*
5. In this position, hold your breath for six to eight seconds.
6. Before you exhale, lift your chin, draw your tongue back in, and close your mouth. Now exhale completely through your nostrils. This completes one round of sitali breathing.

Practice the sitali pranayama for two or three minutes, or until you feel comfortable.

In the beginning, the inhalation-exhalation ratio should be 4:6. After a few days, extend this to 4:8, 5:10, or 6:12.

YOGA AND PRANAYAMA

For the practice of pranayama to be more effective, it is important to know how to control the body through yoga poses or asanas.

Imagine a bottle of water. The water is the prana, and the bottle is the physical body. The water's stillness depends on the bottle's balance. If the bottle is not stable, the water will get shaken up. Likewise, the prana will not be stable through pranayama unless the physical body is stable. Asanas help the body achieve stability.

In the next chapter we will discuss modern yoga and its impact on our energy flow at a physical level.

Yoga

....

Uniting Body, Mind, and Spirit

In its early days, yoga focused on meditation, breathwork, and visualization, though today it is known in the West for its many asanas, which give the body flexibility and vigor, allowing energy to flow through it.

We find the foundations of yoga in the Vedas, the sacred Hindu texts, specifically in the Upanishads. The texts dedicated to this set of practices were written in Sanskrit between 800 and 500 BC, though their sources go back to the north of India five thousand years ago.

How did yoga evolve into what it is today?

The Western Version

As the scholar Mark Singleton explains in his book *Yoga Body*, it was Scandinavian gymnastics that forever changed yoga.

At the end of the nineteenth century, Swedish and Danish gymnastics had revolutionized the way Europeans exercised, even becoming the basis of physical training in military schools all over the continent. The fever for Scandinavian gymnastics also reached India, and by 1920 it was the most popular form of exercise in the country.

It was from this combination of body worship and the meditation tradition that yoga as we know it today emerged.

Swami Vishnudevananda, a disciple of yoga guru Swami Sivananda, was also responsible for the spread of yoga in the West. Arriving in California in 1957, he founded ashrams and yoga centers all over the United States, Canada, and even Europe and New Zealand.

According to him, yoga consists of five basic pillars:

- asanas (physical poses)
- breathwork (pranayama)
- relaxation (savasana)
- a vegetarian diet
- positive thinking and meditation (vedanta and dhyana)

When practicing yoga, we should not focus all our attention on physical flexibility. The ultimate goal of yoga is inner balance and mental peace. In Sanskrit, the word *jyog* means "union" or "connection"; the goal of yoga is to unite body, mind, and spirit.

ACROYOGA

As its name suggests, acroyoga combines yoga with acrobatics. It was developed in the early twenty-first century in the United States and Canada, though there is a video of the Indian yoga guru Tirumalai Krishnamacharya doing acroyoga with a little boy in 1938.

Two people are always needed to practice acroyoga. The first person is called the base, and their role is to provide a foundation for the second person, the flyer. The flyer will perform the most complicated poses, while the base holds them up with their legs, arms, or both.

Practicing Down Dog

Downward-facing dog, or *adho mukha svanasana* in Sanskrit, is one of the most basic and widely practiced asanas.

Beyond its multiple benefits for the back and the general

flexibility of the body, it is one of the simplest poses, perfect for any level of practice.

After doing it for a few minutes, alternating with other asanas to prevent too much blood from rushing to your head, you will improve your blood pressure while exercising the muscles in your limbs. Your spine will also be stretched, reducing pain in your shoulders and your lumbar and cervical areas, and lowering your stress level.

Let's practice the downward-facing dog asana. Although it is one of the simplest asanas, it takes a little concentration to do it well without hurting ourselves:

1. To begin, get down on all fours on your yoga mat, with your hands and knees resting on the floor. Breathe in.

2. Lift your hips up and pull them back until you are in the position of an upside-down V. Exhale.

3. Breathe in as you press into the mat with your hands, keeping your fingers separated. Make sure your hands are in a straight line with your hips and feet. Your hands should feel like a strong base, and your weight should be evenly distributed between your hands and feet.

4. Exhale, concentrating on your heels. Ideally, your heels should be touching the ground, so that your feet are completely flat. This is not easy to do if you are a beginner, so it's okay to keep your heels a little elevated or to bend your knees slightly. Every day you should make an effort to bring your heels closer to the mat. You can remain in this position for thirty seconds, breathing in and out rhythmically.

5. Next, bend your knees and lower yourself to the ground to go back to your original position on all fours.

6. Now you can incorporate a cat pose, with your back arched.

7. Continue with the cow pose, bending your back low. Then repeat the process, returning to downward-facing dog.

8. When you have done as many repetitions as you think you need, you can leave the asana, passing through the position on all fours.

9. Finally, fold forward onto your knees, into *balasana* or child's pose. Hold this pose, touching your forehead to the mat.

Ayurveda

....

Ancestral Medicine

L ike yoga, Ayurveda was developed in India five thousand years ago, and has its roots in the Vedic texts.
This system of traditional Indian medicine is focused on balancing energy in the body to prevent illness. Translated from Sanskrit, *ayur* means "life" and *veda* means "knowledge," so *Ayurveda* literally means "life knowledge," or "wisdom."

The Three Doshas

According to Ayurveda, each person has three different *doshas*—sometimes translated as "humors"—called *vata*, *kapha*, and *pitta*. One of the three is always more present than the others.

Depending on which is more dominant, the body will require different foods, physical exercise, and even different psychological care in order to function optimally. "The *doshas* are like an energy enneagram," explains Guady Ruiz-Giménez Aguilar in *The Art of Ageing Beautifully*. "If you go to see a Hindu doctor or therapist, they will identify your dominant dosha and give you the appropriate health and diet guidelines based on it."

According to Ayurveda, the doshas correspond to five elements: earth, water, air, fire, and ether.

Vata is air and ether.

Kapha is earth and water.

Pitta is fire and water.

Next, we will see what each of the doshas is like so we can identify our own and learn how to take care of them to avoid imbalances. In general, vata is associated with a thin body, pitta with a medium body, and kapha with a heavy body, but there are many more nuances. Let's have a look at each.

The Vata Dosha

Air and ether move energy, and in the body, vata is the energy that moves the breath, the blood, and bodily waste.

Vata people are curious, intelligent, and quick-minded.

They are always moving and love trying new things. They are so creative that their passion for life inspires others. Not content to follow a single path, they want to pursue everything and usually do so successfully.

If they are balanced, then they are enthusiastic, creative, flexible, and full of initiative. An excess of vata, however, can cause insomnia, anxiety, and difficulty dealing with stress. Vata people may blame themselves for things that are not their fault and end up feeling miserable.

Physically, they are thin, small-framed, and agile. Too much vata in the body can cause fatigue, weakness, hypertension, constipation, weight loss, or digestive problems.

Since vata is a combination of air and ether, in excess it can overstimulate the movement of energy, like a wind that sweeps through a house and destroys it. This can be corrected by establishing fixed meal routines and slowing down with meditation.

The Vata Diet

The vata tendency to always be on the move can often lead to these people neglecting their diet and skipping meals, causing them to lose weight and putting their health and energy out of balance.

Eating three nutritious meals a day, always on the same schedule, is essential for sustaining a vata's level of constant activity and maintaining their equilibrium. Let's see which foods in particular are beneficial for them.

RECOMMENDED	NOT RECOMMENDED
Healthful fats and oils (ghee, extra virgin olive oil)	Legumes
Rice, wheat	Tofu
Low-fat dairy products, warm milk	Raw, dry, or cold foods
Nuts, cooked greens, dense fruits such as bananas, avocados, coconut	Bitter foods
Warm herbs and spices such as oregano, cardamom, basil, thyme	Caffeine
Hot, cooked foods	
Sweet foods	

The Vata Lifestyle

For vatas, it is essential to stick to routines and maintain a balanced lifestyle for health and well-being. It is also important not to get cold, which means getting enough sleep and avoiding dry climates and air conditioning.

According to experts, it can be helpful to listen to classical music and to refrain from grueling physical activity. Having a humidifier at home is also recommended.

Vatas get tired easily and are liable to lose weight, which makes exhausting cardio activities unsuitable. Ideal sports for vatas include golf, tennis, tai chi, yoga, and dance, as well as light walking or cycling in flat areas.

The Kapha Dosha

Made up of earth and water, kapha is malleable and cohesive, like clay. In the body, it is the energy that unites cells, bones, muscles, and fat.

An excess of kapha can be a drag on the body's energy. This imbalance must be corrected to ensure movement and fluidity.

Someone with dominant kapha dosha is a compassionate person to whom you tell all your problems, but who keeps their own problems to themselves. They find it difficult to express their feelings. They are a born helper and a lifelong friend.

Kaphas are loving, calm, and considerate. If they are balanced, they are loyal, steadfast, and fun-loving. An excess of kapha, however, can cause feelings of insecurity, attachment, and depression.

Physically, people with a primarily kapha constitution are strong and exhibit qualities related to moisture: dewy eyes; healthy, oily skin and hair. If they are balanced, they have good digestion and healthy sleep patterns. An excess of kapha, on the other hand, can cause lung and weight problems, colds, excess mucus, and thyroid problems. They also tend to have cold extremities.

The Kapha Diet

RECOMMENDED	NOT RECOMMENDED
Light and dry hot foods	Dairy products
Barley, rye, buckwheat	Nuts
Dried fruit	Seeds
Fruits and vegetables	Red meat
Hot spices	Fatty foods
Extra virgin olive oil, ghee	

The Kapha Lifestyle

For kaphas, it is important for meals to be calm and peaceful, with no stress or surprises that might cause an imbalance.

Given that kaphas need movement, dynamic exercise such as aerobics or another kind of cardio is recommended.

It is also important for kaphas not to stagnate mentally. Activities that stimulate them on an intellectual level are highly beneficial.

Everyone, and Kaphas in particular, should take care to stay warm and dry, and avoid being cold or wet.

The Pitta Dosha

Fire and water cancel each other out and evaporate, so in the body, pitta is energy that is transformed. People in whom this dosha is dominant are active and have an athletic build and lots of energy. They sleep little but deeply.

Pittas are passionate, have sharp intellects, and are capable of intense concentration. If they are balanced, they are good at making decisions and are great speakers and teachers. They can be born leaders.

An excess of pitta, however, will cause them to argue about everything and be easily irritated. They can become controlling and prejudiced.

Physically, pittas are medium-size and have good muscle tone. And they exhibit qualities related to heat: baldness or red hair, exuberance, strong sexual desire, warm body temperature, and a hearty appetite.

If they are balanced, they will have excellent digestion and clear skin. An excess of pitta can cause inflammation, indigestion, ulcers, and skin breakouts.

Psychologically, a handicap of the pitta dosha is that they are easily irritated. This excess of inner heat can make them develop acne, moles, or freckles. In a state of imbalance, they may suffer from insomnia and digestive problems.

Due to their direct manner, they can come off as rude when they speak.

The Pitta Diet

RECOMMENDED	NOT RECOMMENDED
Herbal teas (rose hip, mint, and chamomile)	Vinegar
Legumes (lentils, chickpeas)	Salted nuts
Sunflower seeds and oil	Alcohol and caffeine
Blueberries, melon	Hard cheese
Kale, broccoli	Tomatoes, garlic, peppers, onions
Cumin, cilantro, fennel (these cool the digestive tract)	Fried, spicy foods
Barley, oats	Cured meats
Refreshing, sweet, and bitter foods	Salty, acidic, or spicy foods
	Dairy products

The Pitta Lifestyle

For people with an excess of pitta, it is essential to lower heat by working to cool and stabilize their energy. They should eat three meals a day and avoid getting too full or snacking between them, since this will increase their inner fire characteristics.

Refreshing sitali breathing, which we examined in the chapter on pranayama, is especially beneficial for the pitta dosha. They also benefit from activities like swimming, meditation, yoga, and walks in nature.

They should be careful with sports that are too competitive, and with sun exposure, since their skin burns easily.

Turmeric: The Golden Spice

Marco Polo was amazed by the variety of spices he found on his travels through present-day India, and in 1280 he described turmeric in his diary: "There is also a vegetable that has all the properties of true saffron, as well as the smell and the color, and yet it is not really saffron."

Back then, the powder extracted from turmeric was practically unknown in the West. Today it has spread all over the world, and in Latin America it is known as poor man's saffron.

Turmeric is a plant from the same family as ginger. It grows in warm regions of the Indian subcontinent and in Southeast Asia. The most valuable part is its root, which, after being boiled and dried, is ground to produce a golden powder.

There is evidence that turmeric began to be used six thousand years ago, and it spread during the Vedic period—from 1500 to 500 BC—not just as a culinary ingredient but also as a dye for clothing and as an element in religious rituals and in medicine, makeup, and cosmetics.

The Healing Power of Turmeric

Turmeric has been used since the beginning of ayurvedic medicine. The tradition attributes to it so many benefits that laboratories have been attempting to verify its properties. Thousands of scientific articles about the properties of turmeric have been published.

Scientists are trying to confirm whether its therapeutic use is justified for afflictions as varied as constipation, kidney stones, arthritic pain, and irregular menstrual cycles. Though definitive conclusions have not yet been reached, turmeric seems to be a powerful antioxidant and anti-inflammatory agent, and to be capable of killing bacteria.

Homemade Turmeric and Ginger Tea

To make this homemade tea, which we regularly enjoy on our travels, all you need to do is mix the ingredients in a bottle or another container and refrigerate it. Once it has rested in the fridge for one day, it is ready to drink.

- Two teaspoons of ground turmeric
- Fresh grated ginger (about 20 grams)
- A pinch of cayenne or chili powder
- A pinch of black pepper
- A spoonful of honey
- Juice of one lemon (or any other citrus)
- 500 milliliters water

Champissage

The Indian Head Massage

Popularly known as *champi*, which means "head massage" in Hindi, *champissage* has been used for more than a thousand years in India for medical purposes, for relaxation, and for the harmonization of energy. It has its roots in Ayurveda, and as such, it helps to align the mind, body, and spirit through balancing energy.

The champi technique initially centered on massaging the scalp and hair, but it has evolved to include the shoulders, neck, and face. This change took place in the early 1970s, when the manual therapist Narendra Mehta traveled to England to study physiotherapy and began to disseminate this ancestral art.

THE MIRACULOUS HANDS
OF A BLIND MAN

Narendra Mehta was blind from the age of one, which gave him a heightened sense of touch. He was a pioneer of champissage in the United Kingdom, where he was welcomed with enthusiasm, and he originated the Indian head massage as we know it today.

Upon his death, his wife, Kundan Mehta, and his son-in-law, Moses Chundi, took over his center in London, which continues to train students from all over the world.

A Maternal Massage

This technique was originally initiated by mothers who massaged their daughters' heads with almond, coconut, or olive oil to give nourishment and vitality to the hair. Over time, it was observed that in addition to revitalizing the hair, it brought many other benefits.

Even today, most Indian children receive daily head massages to keep them healthy.

The practice was taken up by Indian barbers, who always give their clients a head massage. And it has now spread to salons all over the world.

If you have ever had a scalp massage while getting your hair washed at a salon, you know it is one of the most pleasant feelings in the world, since it relaxes the areas most vulnerable to tension and stress: the upper back, shoulders, neck, head, and face.

But it also manages to relax all the muscles in the body, like a kind of cranial reflexology, conferring a feeling of well-being that begins with the head and moves through the whole body.

In fact, champi stimulates healing in different parts of the body through pressure points on the skull. Massaging the right area can relieve pain caused by stress and can diminish signs of fatigue.

General Benefits

- Relaxes muscles
- Relieves chronic stiffness in neck and shoulders
- Stimulates and improves the lymphatic system
- Improves circulation, bringing more oxygen to the brain
- Restores range of movement and joint flexibility
- Relieves tension headaches, visual fatigue, earaches, jaw pain, sinusitis and congestion, insomnia, and sleep disorders

- Stimulates hair growth
- Increases relaxation and improves sleep quality

Psychological Benefits

- Calm, peace, and tranquility
- Reduced anxiety
- Higher levels of concentration
- A clearer and sharper mind
- Relief from mental fatigue, anxiety, and stress

Subtle Benefits

- Balances energy in the body
- Frees stagnant energy
- Provides general energy healing

How to Give an Indian Head Massage

The process of giving an Indian head massage is simple—anyone can learn to do it. While you can massage yourself, it's more effective to take turns with your partner or a friend, so that the person receiving the massage can be completely relaxed.

Let's see how to practice champi on someone.

1. The person receiving the massage should be sitting comfortably, with the shoulders straight but not tense.

2. Place your hands on the back of the neck. Let them rest there while the massage recipient relaxes.

3. To begin the massage, apply light pressure with your fingers to the base of the skull. Gently turn the head from side to side.

4. Next, make long strokes over the scalp with the fingers of both hands. The massage begins at the base of the skull and progresses to the area behind the ears. Keep massaging the head with circular movements.

5. Most people assume that the temple is the area between the outer corner of the eye and the ear, but in fact it includes the part of the forehead above the ear. Massage this whole area in a clockwise direction, making deep, slow strokes.

6. Play with the hair and comb it with your fingertips, then stroke the head gently with your palms, from the base of the skull to the crown.

7. Rest your forearm on the right side of the person's neck and press downward. After about three seconds, slide your forearm down the cervical spine until it reaches the right shoulder.

8. Do the same on the left side. This part of the massage eliminates tension in the cervical spine, which makes it excellent for reducing accumulated stress.

Tantra

....

The Sacred Encounter

The earliest known tantric texts date from between 300 and 400 AD and were written in India, in the bosom of the Hindu and Buddhist traditions. They were poetic metaphors on unity and divine love, with special attention to the sacred union of masculinity and femininity.

In Sanskrit, the word *tantra* means "net," "weaving," or even "interwoven." A common mistake is to associate tantra with uninhibited sexual experiences, when in reality it is a combination of sexuality, spirituality, and mindfulness or full attention.

The Temples of Khajuraho

In central India, in the district of Chhatarpur, Madhya Pradesh, lies Khajuraho, a group of monuments named a

UNESCO World Heritage Site in 1986. Of the eighty-five temples built before the twelfth century, only about twenty remain standing today, most of them Hindu. Of those surviving temples, most are dedicated to Shiva and Vishnu.

Khajuraho was one of the birthplaces of tantra. The walls of its temples bear witness to this, their explicit erotic sculptures attracting thousands of tourists every year.

While 90 percent of the wall art represents symbolic values and daily scenes from the Indian society of the period, the remaining 10 percent are of a sensual and erotic nature. Even today there is no consensus on what they are meant to convey.

For some, they are deities connecting with one another through sexual activity. For others, the sculptures are an ode to tantra, and the figures do not represent anyone in particular, but rather are simply meant to inspire. Many of the positions seem to be drawn from the *Kama Sutra*, a very popular text and one of the most important in the Indian tradition.

In these intricately carved statues, one can see sexually explicit acts between people of all types of orientations.

TABOO-FREE SEX

In the Indian society of the tenth century, which still had not been influenced by Christianity or Islam, sexual relations were seen as just one expression of daily life. The sculptures that today we find shocking might have been for them simply a representation of natural acts related to fertility.

Weaving the Physical and the Spiritual Together

Tantra reached its height in the eleventh and twelfth centuries, when it became extremely popular in India. In response to the idea that liberation could be achieved only through a renunciation of the worldly and through rigorous asceticism, tantric yogis posited that human suffering arises from the erroneous notion of separation and argued for a celebration of the sensual and thus for physical transcendence.

Mens sana in corpore sano—a healthy mind in a healthy body—could easily have been their slogan.

The goal of tantra is to achieve a sensual experience, honoring the body from the place of the soul. Tantric sex seeks to "weave together" the physical with the spiritual, strengthening the experience of intimacy. Although tantra is more often practiced as a couple, it can also be experienced alone.

The practice of tantra is slow and unhurried, with long sessions and with patience as an essential element. The objective is to achieve an intense but conscious connection with your partner or yourself. To achieve this, breathing techniques, sounds, movements, and meditation are used to activate sexual energy.

Contrary to popular belief, genital contact or sexual intercourse do not have to be part of tantric sex. In fact, practitioners try to postpone this to enjoy the sensuality and full attention for as long as possible.

Let's look at three basic exercises for practicing tantra as a couple:

1. **Eye contact**

   A good way of exploring the world of tantra with your partner is to strengthen your eye contact. Looking deeply into each other's eyes, coupled with deep breathing, helps you connect while at the same time stimulating each person's sexual energy.

1. Sit face-to-face with your partner in a pleasant, peaceful place, in a position that is comfortable for both of you. You can sit on the bed with your legs crossed, or even in two chairs facing each other. You can do this first exercise fully clothed.

2. Start by gazing straight into your partner's eyes while your partner does the same. Get lost in their pupils, as if they were the true doors to their soul.

3. Breathe consciously, slowly, and deeply, inhaling and exhaling through your nose, trying to synchronize your breath with your partner's. The aim is to connect with the person in front of you until you are breathing together, at the same time.

4. Continue like this for a few minutes, maintaining eye contact. At the same time, focus on the feeling awakened inside you, especially around your navel and just below it. According to tantra, this is where kundalini energy comes from. This energy is hot

and rises from the navel up through the torso, flooding the upper part of the body with warmth, sensuality, and energy.

5. Once you are feeling this, you can start to undress and/or touch your partner however you like, always maintaining eye contact and keeping your breathing synchronized. Feel your partner and rediscover them from this place of full attention.

Enjoy the shared moment and all the new sensations that arise in the heightened state of consciousness that this exercise promotes.

2. **Conscious sensuality**

The mindfulness we will see in the next chapter is a requirement for practicing tantra. Full attention is essential when it comes to relating to your partner during tantric sex.

A good conscious exercise for heightening sensuality can be done using a timer.

• Set a timer for exactly five minutes to touch your partner with absolute concentration. Everything you do should be done with the utmost amazement, taking delight in everything you see, as if it were the first time. Be thankful for the chance to be intimate with your partner and focus on every single detail as you touch them.

- After five minutes, switch roles. Now it is your partner's turn to touch your face, torso, arms, and legs while you keep your eyes open and intensely absorb each caress.

The goal of this sensual awareness exercise is to be completely present when touching or being touched. Being here and now heightens your own sensations while also empowering your partner in their own body, since you are communicating to them that nothing is more important than this shared moment.

3. **The art of slowness**

Among other things, tantra is synonymous with patience and slowness. Life is a journey and not a destination. There is no rush, and no one should force themselves. A couple practicing tantric sex tries to delay orgasm as long as possible, thus experiencing sensuality in a state of calm and presence.

- When having sex with your partner, try to make the movements slow and rhythmic. Enjoy the connection with your partner without thinking of anything else.

You and your partner should be in control of time rather than time controlling you. Einstein showed that time is relative, and perhaps tantra is an opportunity to experience that for yourself.

Meditation

The Origin of Mindfulness

Those who understand the workings of the mind know that happiness is found not in objects or external circumstances but in the clarity of our inner lens.

A mind full of prejudice and preconceived ideas that looks back with pain and resentment and forward with fear and anxiety does not allow us to enjoy the happiness of the here and now.

Fortunately, human beings have a tool to free themselves from all this mental noise, a cleanser or solvent for the impurities clouding the lens through which we perceive the world. And this tool, practiced in India for thousands of years by numerous spiritual traditions, is called meditation.

Three or four decades ago in the West, meditation was associated with Zen, the Japanese branch of Buddhism with centers in thousands of cities all over the world. Sitting in front of a wall to calm the mind became a fashionable practice that gave rise to books like *The Empty Mirror* by Janwillem van de Wetering and films like *Enlightenment Guaranteed* by the German director Doris Dörrie.

Beginning in the 1990s, however, Zen was surpassed in popularity by mindfulness. But it is essentially the same. It is about sitting with your mind in order to free it from suffering.

JON KABAT-ZINN'S KARMIC MISSION

Jon Kabat-Zinn, a native New Yorker with a doctorate in molecular biology, is responsible for the rise of mindfulness. Thanks to him, meditation techniques have taken hold in the secular world and even in businesses.

After spending his youth protesting the Vietnam War, he began to search for his purpose in life, his purushartha, which in those days he called his karmic mission. To do so, he trained in meditation with Philip Kapleau, a Buddhist missionary who gave a talk at MIT, where Kabat-Zinn was a student. He later deepened his meditation practice with Buddhist teachers such as Thich Nhat Hanh and the Korean Zen master Seung-sahn.

Interested in bringing the benefits of meditation to

the medical field, in 1979 Kabat-Zinn founded the Stress Reduction Clinic, where he began to apply what he had learned in his spiritual practice, detaching it from the Buddhist realm. There he created the celebrated, scientifically based Mindfulness-Based Stress Reduction (MBSR) program. He would begin to have a major impact with his book *Full Catastrophe Living*, in which he detailed the practice of mindfulness.

Kabat-Zinn had found his karmic mission.

Now we will look at three meditations, two of them with Indian roots.

Kirtan, the Chanting Meditation

The kirtan, or chanting of mantras, is a kind of meditation done aloud and in movement. Far from the silence of full attention or the austerity of Zen, here instruments, voices, applause, and dances are all mixed together by the participants. Kirtan is ideal for practicing in a group, though it is also possible to perform this meditation at home while listening to or watching an online session.

The chanting of mantras is very common in ashrams in India. The master of ceremonies directs the meditation, chanting mantras for the others to answer in a call-and-response.

In kirtan, anything goes: moving your body to the rhythm of the music, closing your eyes, crying, slapping your chest with your hands . . . In fact, this active meditation encourages uninhibited physical expression, freeing the energy of the whole body while the blessings of the mantra being sung are received.

OM NAMAH SHIVAYA is a mantra often used in kirtan. It is one of the best-known in Hinduism and the most important in Shivaism. It means literally, "adoration of Shiva."

This meditation, far from leaving you relaxed, is perfect for lifting your mood and energy levels. Starting your day with a kirtan session on YouTube is a wonderful idea, though it can also dispel tension in your body after the workday.

Meditating with Visualization

Tibetan Buddhism includes visualization practices through which meditators seek to develop positive qualities like compassion and goodwill by imagining themselves and others as benevolent beings.

To introduce you to this kind of practice, centered on the wise and loving presence of Siddhartha Gautama himself, you can use a Buddha figure to support your meditation. We will show you step-by-step.

1. Sit in a comfortable position with your legs crossed, or if you can, in lotus position. If you have back problems, you can sit in a chair.

2. Close your eyes and imagine the Buddha floating in front of you, emanating a golden light. This light is warm and loving, and as it reaches you, it fills you with compassion, goodness, and health. Feel how universal love penetrates you through your crown, your third eye, and all the pores in your body.

3. While this divine energy flows inside you, the negative energies accumulated in your body no longer have any place, so picture them leaving your body in the form of a black or gray smoke, flowing down to your feet and becoming part of Mother Earth, which absorbs and transforms them.

4. Continue the meditation until you feel that the Buddha's compassionate light has filled you completely, emptying you of the dark energy you had

inside. This regenerative meditation restores your natural wholeness and well-being.

MINIMUM AGREEMENT WITH YOURSELF

On one of our trips to Asia together, the authors of this book made a habit of performing the compassion meditation every night before going to bed. It was very helpful as a way to fix a point of departure for the kind of life we want to live.

To calm the body and mind, by the light of just one candle we repeated the mantra OM MANI PADME HUM. When we felt that our minds finally resembled a placid lake, one of us spoke this desire aloud:

"If I am not capable of making others happy, let my actions at least not be an obstacle to their happiness."

Voicing this minimal agreement, night after night, has been an important compass in our imperfect lives.

Explore Your Body through Meditation

The third technique in this chapter is a basic aspect of each of the mindfulness practices we have already discussed. The body scan is an excellent way to come back to the here and now after the general disconnection we experience due in part to screens and to information overload.

The goal of this meditation is to return your attention to yourself and to what is happening to you on a physical level. Focusing on the sensations you experience in your body is a good way to center the mind and prevent it from wandering aimlessly. Let's practice.

1. Sit in a chair with your back straight, your shoulders relaxed, and your feet flat on the floor. Your legs should be bent at the knees at a ninety-degree angle. Alternatively, this meditation can be done lying on your back in a savasana position, but be careful not to fall asleep.

2. Breathe in slowly and deeply and focus all your attention on the toes of your left foot. Are they comfortable? Squeezed together? Are they cold? Hot? Are they sweaty? Dry? Go through your toes one by one, from your little toe to your big one, continuing on to the sole of your foot, your heel, ankle, lower leg, knee, and thigh.

3. Repeat the exercise with the right side of your body.

4. When you get to your pelvis, direct your attention to your glutes and hips, then go up to the area around your navel. As you travel up your body, relax your muscles, making the meditation not just a training in complete attention but also a physical and emotional relaxation.

5. After the chest, focus on the back, then scan down from the left shoulder to the fingertips, and do the same with the right arm.

6. Finally, focus on the back of your neck, your head, and all your facial muscles.

NOTE: It is normal for your mind to wander at some point, and you should not beat yourself up about it. When you notice this happening, return your attention lovingly to the meditation and continue with the exercise. Being aware of when the mind is drifting is the first step to controlling it.

Epilogue

Great Souls Are Like Clouds

As we finish this book, the "Raag Shivanjali" by Hariprasad Chaurasia plays on our stereo. For a long time, we have shared a passion for this Indian flute master. His music transports us to another dimension, where the divine and the human dance and interweave like the sculptures at Khajuraho.

In Sanskrit, *raga* means "color" but also "mood." Without a doubt, what this delicate piece by Chaurasia evokes in us is serenity.

India had always been an oasis in our imagination, nurtured first by the stories of Rudyard Kipling and later by those of holy men and gurus, until we were able to travel there, and our amazement was multiplied.

As long as the essence of India exists, there is hope for human beings beyond a world of mundane transactions.

Around the fifth century, in this luminous part of the planet, there was a poet and playwright called Kalidasa, which means servant of Kali, the goddess of creation, change, destruction, death, and time.

We would like to close this book with a line attributed to this author that has always fascinated us: "Great souls are like clouds: they gather in order to pour."

What a beautiful encapsulation of India, the cradle of spirituality. As we look toward the future, we hope that India's time-tested path to happiness inspires every day of your life.

The Ten Indian Laws of Happiness

Before we say goodbye, let's take with us as a souvenir ten laws to remember the age-old wisdom we have been getting to know throughout this book.

1. **Live according to the four purusharthas.** When in doubt, in times of trouble or when you are feeling lost, come back to review your lifestyle through the lenses of the four purusharthas, or goals of human life: Are you doing the right things for your people without expectation of rewards (dharma)? Are you enjoying your time and appreciating the beauty of the world (kama)? Are you generating wealth and prosperity (artha)? Are you learning more about yourself and working on your self-realization (moksha)?

2. **Learn from those who know.** It can be a teacher, a guru, a book, anything that inspires you and takes

you beyond yourself. Human beings may have a beginning, but they have no end. Your horizon is wherever you set your sights.

3. **Let go of everything you don't need.** Follow the example of the sadhus and dare to travel light, knowing that there is nothing important that you could lose. Wherever you go, you are with yourself. What more could you need?

4. **Create your own ashram.** Your life project needs an inner circle that will empower you, especially when hard times come and hope wanes. Choose your fellow travelers well.

5. **Live mindfully.** Whether through meditation, yoga, or flow, live whatever you are doing fully. Eliminate distractions. Dare to be present with a single thing that contains the whole Universe.

6. **Know yourself.** The Greeks from the Axial Age and the wise men of India in every era said so. *Who am I?* Ramana Maharshi made his disciples ask themselves in order to cultivate their fourth purushartha (moksha). Are you bold enough to explore yourself?

7. **Put an end to vicious cycles.** Cultivating the first purushartha (dharma) will allow you to stop

THE TEN INDIAN LAWS OF HAPPINESS

repeating the errors holding you back. Do what is right and be generous with the world and with yourself, and good karma will flood your life with light.

8. **Breathe!** Your energy, your serenity, and the days given to you to enjoy all depend on the air that enters and leaves your lungs. Practice pranayama. Your life literally depends on it!

9. **Feed your body, mind, and spirit.** Everything is connected, so none of these should be neglected. Nourish yourself with Ayurveda, practice tantra and yoga, calm your mind, and set out on a path to paradise.

10. **Live in the moment.** We spend 80 percent of our time thinking about the past and the future. Invest your energy in the present, which is the home of happiness.

Let's believe in the impossible and make our lives into a garden where the best of everyone can flourish.

With all our wishes for your happiness, thank you for joining us on this journey.

HÉCTOR GARCÍA AND FRANCESC MIRALLES

Acknowledgments

···

To Marta Sevilla and the Urano family, the original publishers of this book in Spain, for continuing to walk with us on this beautiful adventure.

To Sandra Bruna, our agent, who has taken our works to more than sixty-five languages.

To our publishers all over the world, for the passion and care you put into your work.

To Yoshiaki, who encouraged us to visit Ogimi, Japan, the "village of longevity," giving rise to everything we have done since then.

To our readers all over the world, with special thanks to those in India. We have received so much affection from you in the past few years that we wanted to devote this new book to you.

To everyone who cultivates their passions and cares for their inner and outer health, their own and that of others.

To all of you, thank you!

Suggestions for Further Reading

Aguilar, Guady Ruiz-Giménez. *The Art of Ageing Beautifully: From Pilates to Mindfulness*. Self-published, 2021.

Armstrong, Karen. *The Great Transformation: The Beginning of Our Religious Traditions*. New York: Anchor Books, 2007.

Buddha. *The Dhammapada*. Translated by Valerie Roebuck. New York: Penguin Classics, 2010.

Csikszentmihalyi, Mihaly. *Flow: The Psychology of Optimal Experience*. New York: Harper Perennial, 2008.

Das, Gurcharan. *India Grows at Night: A Liberal Case for a Strong State*. Delhi: Penguin India, 2012.

Frankl, Viktor E. *Man's Search for Ultimate Meaning*. New York: Basic Books, 2000.

García, Héctor. *A Geek in Japan: Discovering the Land of Manga, Anime, Zen, and the Tea Ceremony*. Clarendon, VT: Tuttle, 2011.

García, Héctor, and Francesc Miralles. *Ikigai: The Japanese Secret to a Long and Happy Life*. New York: Penguin Books, 2017.

García, Héctor, and Francesc Miralles. *The Ikigai Journey*. Clarendon, VT: Tuttle, 2020.

Gilbert, Elizabeth. *Eat, Pray, Love: One Woman's Search for Everything across Italy, India and Indonesia*. New York: Riverhead Books, 2007.

Goleman, Daniel. *Emotional Intelligence: Why It Can Matter More Than IQ.* New York: Bantam, 2006.

Jaspers, Karl. *The Origin and Goal of History.* London: Routledge, 2021.

Kabat-Zinn, Jon. *Full Catastrophe Living: Using the Wisdom of Your Body and Mind to Face Stress, Pain, and Illness.* New York: Bantam, 2013.

Kerouac, Jack. *On the Road.* New York: Penguin Classics, 2008.

Mariwala, Harsh, and Ram Charan. *Harsh Realities: The Making of Marico.* Delhi: Portfolio India, 2021.

Miralles, Francesc. *Los lobos cambian el río (The Wolves Change the River).* Barcelona: Ediciones Obelisco, 2021.

Parsons, Tony. *All There Is.* Shaftesbury, UK: Open Secret Publishing, 2013.

Ruiz, Don Miguel. *The Four Agreements: A Practical Guide to Personal Freedom.* San Rafael, CA: Amber-Allen, 1997.

Russell, Bertrand. *The Conquest of Happiness.* New York: Liveright, 2013.

Singleton, Mark. *Yoga Body: The Origins of Modern Posture Practice.* Oxford, UK: Oxford University Press, 2010.

St. James, Elaine. *Simplify Your Life: 100 Ways to Slow Down and Enjoy the Things That Really Matter.* Glendale, CA: Hyperion, 1994.

Sylvester, Richard. *I Hope You Die Soon: Words on Non-Duality.* Oakland, CA: Non-Duality Press, 2017.

Tharoor, Shashi. *Why I Am a Hindu.* London: Scribe, 2018.

Tolle, Eckhart. *The Power of Now: A Guide to Spiritual Enlightenment.* Novato, CA: New World Library, 2004.

van de Wetering, Janwillem. *The Empty Mirror: Experiences in a Japanese Zen Monastery.* New York: St. Martin's Griffin, 1999.